Turner as Professor
THE ARTIST AND LINEAR PERSPECTIVE

MAURICE DAVIES

Turner as Professor
THE ARTIST AND LINEAR PERSPECTIVE

TATE GALLERY

EXHIBITION AND CATALOGUE SPONSORED BY VOLKSWAGEN

cover
'George IV at St Giles's, Edinburgh' c.1822 (detail, fig.119)

ISBN 1 85437 103 7

Published by order of the Trustees 1992
on the occasion of the exhibition at the Tate Gallery
7 October 1992 – 31 January 1993
Designed by Caroline Johnston
Published by Tate Gallery Publications, Millbank, London SW1P 4RG
© Tate Gallery and the author 1992 All rights reserved
Typeset in Baskerville by Status Graphics, London
Printed and bound in Great Britain by Westerham Press,
Edenbridge, Kent on 150gsm Parilux matt

CONTENTS

7   Foreword

9   Sponsor's Foreword

10   The Turner Scholarships

11   Acknowledgments

13   Editorial Note

15   CHAPTER 1 Professor of Perspective
    Perspective in Early Nineteenth-Century Britain [16]
    Professorial Preparations [18]
    Revisions and Repeats [21]
    The Lecture Diagrams [22]
    Poor Performance: Adverse Reactions [26]

31   CHAPTER 2 Turner's 1811 Lectures
    Lecture 1: The Importance of Perspective and Geometry [31]
    Lecture 2: Standard Perspective and its Problems [36]
    Lectures 3 and 4: Practical Perspective Techniques [43]
    Lecture 5: Rules for Reflection and Refraction [50]
    Lecture 6: Landscape Painting Reviewed [54]

57   CHAPTER 3 Painter of Perspective
    Ignorance or Indifference? Turner's Practical Perspective Skills [57]
    The Foundation of Art: Perspective in the Design of Turner's Pictures [63]
    Perspective for Grandeur and Elevation [67]
    'Attaining Apparent Altitude' [71]
    'Only One Horizontal in Nature' [75]
    Turner's Welcoming Foregrounds [77]
    Rejecting Rectilinearity [82]
    'Rome from the Vatican' [85]
    'The Limits of Extended Sight': Petworth Park [91]
    Variant Views: Vortices and Vignettes [98]
    Indifferent or Inspired? Turner's Attitude to Linear Perspective [102]

114 Glossary

115 Select Bibliography

116 List of Works

123 Index

FOREWORD

On 10 December 1807 Turner was elected professor of perspective at the Royal Academy, but it was not until January 1811 that he gave his first course of six lectures. During these three years Turner carried out extensive research in preparation for these lectures. He continued to lecture until 1828 to mixed critical response.

In 1991 Maurice Davies was appointed a Turner Scholar, the third to be supported by Volkswagen, in order to pursue his researches into the lectures which had been previously so little studied. This book has been published on the occasion of an exhibition held at the Tate Gallery to illustrate the results of his research.

Mr Davies looks at the way Turner thought about perspective when arranging his compositions and how he manipulated it for his own needs. He considers the lectures themselves, including the extensive preparatory work, and illustrates his text with examples of the many diagrams that Turner produced to accompany the lectures. He also examines the way the lectures developed in later years and summarises some of Turner's key attitudes to linear perspective.

All the diagrams for Turner's lectures are in the Turner Bequest, but manuscripts for the lectures for the most part belong to the British Library. Thanks to the generosity of owners we have been able to supplement the exhibition with a few important loans.

I should like to thank Maurice Davies for all his work. He has a deep interest in the lectures and in Turner's approach to perspective which he conveys with great enthusiasm. We are grateful to him for his painstaking research into this rather unfamiliar area of Turner's work.

Finally I want to thank Volkswagen for sponsoring this third Turner Scholar. Without such generous and far-sighted support much-needed new Turner research could not be achieved.

Nicholas Serota
Director

SPONSOR'S FOREWORD

Turner as Professor: The Artist and Linear Perspective marks the third exhibition and publication in the Volkswagen Turner Scholarship series. Our objective with these scholarships is to provide the necessary resources for original research into the extraordinary genius of Joseph Mallord William Turner.

Maurice Davies's work on Turner's use of linear perspective certainly gives us an opportunity to view Turner from a fresh standpoint. The exploration of the artist's approach to conventional and manipulative perspective, in terms of experimentation, accuracy and balance, is compelling.

Not only does it shed fresh light on Turner himself, it illustrates the diverse nature of the research of the Volkswagen Scholars. Previous exhibitions and catalogues have involved Dr Cecilia Powell's study of Turner's sketching tours along the great rivers of Europe, preceded by Peter Bower's exposition of Turner's use of paper.

Maurice Davies's reconstruction of Turner's perspective lectures at the Royal Academy aptly demonstrates another facet of the scholarships – the ability to create a legacy of added knowledge.

My gratitude and that of my company goes to Maurice Davies for his enthusiasm, effort and research scholarship. Our thanks must also go to all involved at the Tate Gallery, particularly Nicholas Serota and Andrew Wilton.

Michael Cornish
Marketing Director
V.A.G. (UK) Limited

THE TURNER SCHOLARSHIPS – SPONSORED BY VOLKSWAGEN

The Turner Scholarships were established by the Tate Gallery in 1988, with the support of Volkswagen, to fund original research by visiting scholars into the works contained in the Turner Bequest at the Tate Gallery. The Scholarships provide an opportunity for scholars to work as 'guest curators', and to prepare an exhibition and publication based on their researches.

Awards are made biennially and in 1988 two Scholars were appointed: Peter Bower and Dr Cecilia Powell. The results of Peter Bower's researches were seen in the successful exhibition *Turner's Papers* which opened at the Tate Gallery in October 1990. Mr Bower, a paper historian, examined Turner's use of paper during the first half of his working life and charted the developing relationship between Turner's materials and his vision of each individual drawing. He is continuing his research into the later years of Turner's life. Dr Cecilia Powell's researches culminated in the exhibition *Turner's Rivers of Europe: The Rhine, Meuse and Mosel* which was shown first at the Tate Gallery in the autumn of 1991 and subsequently in Brussels and Bonn. She has now started new research into Turner's travels in Germany.

Two further Scholars were appointed in November 1990: Mr Maurice Davies and Dr Jan Piggott. Dr Jan Piggott is studying the vignettes engraved after Turner and prepared by him to illustrate works of literature. His work will lead to an exhibition and publication in the autumn of 1993. Maurice Davies's work on the perspective lectures given by Turner at the Royal Academy between 1811 and 1828 is the subject of this book and of the present exhibition.

ACKNOWLEDGMENTS

In ten years of research into Turner's perspective lectures I have benefited from the help of many broadminded institutions and individuals. If Warwick University's undergraduate course in pure mathematics (leading to either a Bachelor of Arts or a Bachelor of Sciences degree – the choice is up to individual graduates) had not been broadminded enough to allow its students a completely free choice of subjects for half of their studies, I would never have taken art history in the first place, and Michael Rosenthal would never have had the chance to send me to the Courtauld Institute – which admitted a mathematician with some knowledge of architectural history but scant idea about painting. At the Courtauld, Michael Kitson felt sure that Turner's lectures were a problem that could have a solution, and has paid for his certainty ever since in supervising my PhD thesis, ably assisted by Martin Kemp. My work was funded generously for three years by the government, first through the Department of Education and Science, and later through the British Academy. The University of London Central Research Fund also made a contribution. But to live a student's life in London was financially challenging even in the early 1980s and I might have been forced into chartered accountancy and away from Turner's lecture manuscripts, without the help of my parents and my wife Nicolina Vinti. As I have lurched from pure maths into art history and museum curatorship (and now magazine editing), they have been unfailingly supportive.

And then came Volkswagen. Their sponsorship of the Turner Scholarship gave me the opportunity to develop my work by investigating Turner's use of perspective in his pictures and to present the results of my research to a wide audience. My employer, the Museums Association, particularly its director, Mark Taylor, was tolerant enough to allow me to work part-time for just over a year to take advantage of Volkswagen's generosity. In my part-time absence I think my staff enjoyed their new-found freedom, and rose to the occasion; allowing me to research on, without too much worry about *Museums Journal* deadlines, page layouts and libel writs. I thank Catrina Lucas, Michael Wright and Christina Ballinger.

Over the twelve months of my scholarship I received advice, encouragement and practical assistance from Peter Bower, Anthea Callen, Cathy Davies, Anne Forsdyke, John Gage, John Murdoch, Jan Piggott, Cecilia Powell, Ursula Seibold, Greg Smith, Jerry Ziff, and members

ACKNOWLEDGMENTS

of the Tate Gallery staff. Others have helped in many ways and I thank them all. Michael Wright, Greg Smith, Ian Warrell, Andrew Wilton, David Brown, Nicolina Vinti and Bob and Frances Davies all improved my text and tightened my sloppy thinking. Lapses that remain are, of course, my own.

Had it not been for the broadmindedness and imaginative thinking of others, I would never have been able to undertake this project. In contrast, the study of art history is riven by often narrow-minded disputes between 'connoisseurs' and 'new art historians'. While these disputes can occasionally be a source of amusement and entertainment to informed observers, they usually benefit no-one, and do nothing to promote the enjoyment and understanding of art to wider publics, an undertaking that surely should be the main aim of exhibitions in public art galleries. I hope I have not fallen into too many academic traps and have been broadminded enough to take advantage of many types of scholarship, without letting them obscure my subject unnecessarily.

Maurice Davies

EDITORIAL NOTE

Quotations from Turner's lecture manuscripts have all been edited: most punctuation has been added; Turner's spelling has been regularised; and his grammar has been selectively improved. His deletions, amendments and other revisions to the lecture manuscripts are not identified: deleted items are simply omitted, and most additions are incorporated without comment. This editing is necessary to avoid drawing undue attention to Turner's style at the expense of his content. However, all words given in quotations do occur in the original manuscripts, with editorial additions always enclosed in square brackets. Any omissions are signified by three dots.

Full details of the illustrations are given in the List of Works (pp.116–21).

MS A, B, C, etc. are references to British Library Additional Manuscript 46151 A, B, C, etc. Some other manuscripts of Turner's lectures remain in a private collection, and I would like to thank their owner for allowing me access to them, and to books used by Turner in preparing his lectures.

Abbreviations

B&J	Martin Butlin and Evelyn Joll, *The Paintings of J.M.W. Turner*, 2 vols., revised ed. 1984
R	W.G. Rawlinson, *The Engraved Work of J.M.W. Turner, R.A.*, 2 vols., 1908 and 1913
TB	A.J. Finberg, *A Complete Inventory of the Drawings of the Turner Bequest*, 2 vols. 1909
W	Andrew Wilton, *The Life and Work of J.M.W. Turner*, 1979 (catalogue of watercolours)
RA	Exhibited at the Royal Academy

For other published material which is abbreviated in the text, see Select Bibliography (p.115).

9

by the Luminary

~~unless the cone~~
is in shadow. in general position
~~Horizontal plane~~
~~on which they stand~~

This in fact throws us back upon some position of artificial Lights and could the mind but place them as it while in the rays used to illuminate the whole world countrys before a Throne by known causes the shade of any two would be similar for its is the approximation of the Eye to the cause of the shadow which certainly makes it equal to the permitted. extends the by the radius but cannot reduce the shadow less than it can be but. Thus few times but nothing relative to position of vision, but the absolute situation of the Eye along the central line equal to the apex of the cone of Rays and bring the supposed light artificial as a lamp natural light as the Sun

If we are looking down the cone of Rays and the eye equal to its Apex, it would ~~be~~ be said to be a right cone for then there would be no Shadow in nature of the Cylinder; ~~but by~~ ~~have addressd~~ the Rules there would in as much of course reverse this and the Cylinder or the transposed rays are drawn unmixed unmoved, one gives ~~Radiated, for the ~~~ light~~ Light and its opposite shade

The Shadows thrown which on two planes intersecting the Shadow shew otherwise would be horizontal either the perpendicular or inclined face of the said planes; The following is from Malton with the overlace of the Shadow by the supposed plane of the sun on the Horizontal, the until it touches the plane, then it runs perpendicular to its face, till they meet. The corresponding Lines returns by the principle of the transposing theory. The second the lines are parallel, the offence will be seen at the top of the figures

Any figure whose Base

CHAPTER 1 PROFESSOR OF PERSPECTIVE

J.M.W. Turner was elected professor of perspective at the Royal Academy General Assembly of 10 December 1807.[1] Although the only candidate, he was well qualified. In the late 1780s he had trained in architectural drawing, partly as a pupil of Thomas Malton Junior (1748–1804), an accomplished architectural draughtsman who was a member of a family which was unusually well versed in perspective. Malton's father, also called Thomas (1726–1801) wrote one of the most comprehensive and elegant treatises on perspective ever published. Brother James also produced a book on the subject, published in 1800.[2] Partly as a result of his early training, Turner was extremely competent in perspective techniques by the time the vacancy for the professorship arose. Since the mid-1790s he had been able to produce remarkably convincing representations of space (see, e.g. figs.66, 95). In addition to his great practical skills, his works demonstrate his strong interest in experimenting with perspective and fully exploiting its potential (e.g. figs.72, 77).

When Turner submitted his candidature for the professorship in March 1807, he was thirty-one years old, he had been a full member of the Royal Academy for five years, and had served on its Council.[3] It was entirely appropriate for him to offer to make a further contribution to the Academy's work and to the development of the arts in Britain. He gave a modest explanation of his motives for taking the post: 'The desire to be useful, or that the situation of a professor in perspective should not pass on unfilled, tempted the offer of my services, although conditional – if no other member offered then I would endeavour to be useful to an institution to which I owe everything. For I cannot look back but with pride and pleasure to that time, the Halcyon perhaps of my days, when I received instruction within these walls; and listened, I hope I did, with a just sense and respect.'[4]

The vacancy also offered Turner a chance to raise his professional status. The constitution of the Royal Academy was clear that only an Academician could be its professor of perspective and, while perspective itself was perhaps an unappealing subject, the post had a high level of prestige. Its importance is indicated by the substantial fee of £60 for each annual course of six lectures. Although Royal Academy lectures were ostensibly for students in the Academy Schools, they were open to all who could obtain an admission ticket (which had to be signed by a Royal Academician) and were reviewed in the press. This gave professors the opportunity to state publicly their artistic

fig.1 Manuscript of one of Turner's perspective lectures, after 1816

fig.2 George Scharf I, 'Westmacott's Lecture at the Royal Academy, Somerset House' c.1830

principles to a wide audience (fig.2). This must have appealed to Turner, who was simultaneously beginning to promote his view of landscape painting in his *Liber Studiorum*.

Sir Joshua Reynolds's seminal annual Discourses when he was President of the Royal Academy demonstrated to Turner that addresses at the Academy could attract great attention and acclaim. To an extent Turner does seem to have hoped to emulate the past President and the young professor's perspective lectures are littered with direct and half-remembered quotations from Reynolds's Discourses. The first lecture included an 'elogium' upon him: 'Sir Joshua left to future art a volume rich, full and inexhaustible; emblazoned by the powerful imagery of his own works and clasped with the strongest tie he could leave: his advice. But it is the lot of all to follow, and mine is a humble one.' Turner spoke of 'adding my feeble voice of gratitude to his memory' and explained: 'I must many times revert to his words and to his works in the course of this enquiry.'[5]

Perspective in Early Nineteenth-Century Britain

As professor of perspective Turner had to bridge the gap between practising artists and the published literature on perspective. Eighteenth- and early nineteenth-century perspective treatises concerned themselves with a mathematically precise system of perspective that was

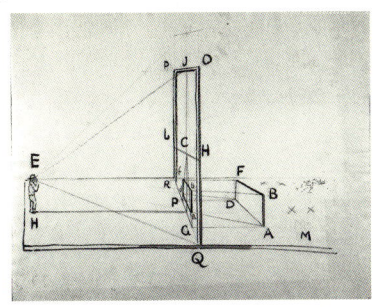

fig.3 'The Geometry of Standard Perspective as the Intersection of the Cone of Vision', lecture diagram c.1816–28

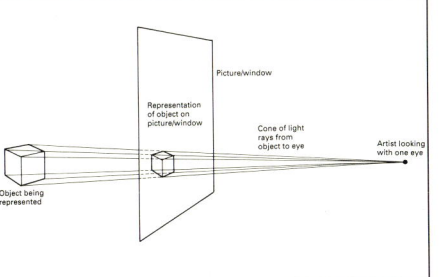

fig.4 A standard perspective representation as an intersection of the cone of vision (modern diagram)

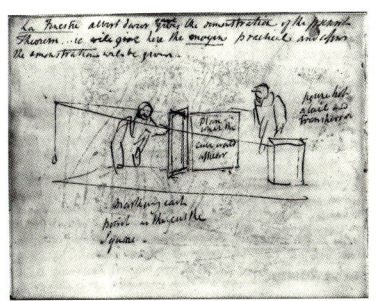

fig.5 *Perspective* sketchbook, 'Dürer's Perspective Fenestre' (taken from Salomon de Caus, *La perspective avec la raison des ombres et mirroirs*, 1612, Tenth Theorem) c.1809

capable of representing objects with complete geometrical accuracy. The version of perspective offered in treatises was highly theoretical. It was complex in its techniques, not least because a great amount of information about the exact dimensions and shapes of each individual object had to be obtained before the process of representation could begin. This information may have been available to architects and architectural draughtsmen, who formed a substantial part of the audience for perspective treatises (and presumably for Royal Academy perspective lectures), but since the middle of the sixteenth century few artists had used full, accurate techniques of perspective. By the early nineteenth century, the theoretical approach to perspective had become increasingly irrelevant to painters.[6]

Artists, particularly landscape painters, also had to contend with the fact that the system of perspective presented in treatises was far removed from the experience of viewing the world with two eyes while moving about. As far as treatises were concerned, artists were supposed to remain motionless, fixed at a single spot, and to view the scene before them with only one eye. They explained that light rays travel to the artist's eye from the object, forming a cone. The picture is then simply a framed intersection of this cone (figs.3, 4). Treatises analysed the geometry of this 'cone of vision' and developed methods and techniques of perspective that were based on a rigorous foundation of Euclidian geometry.

Since Alberti's *De Pictura*, written in 1435, this system of perspective as the intersection of the cone of vision had been presented as a view through a window, and in some treatises, such as Dürer's (fig.5), it was shown as such. This was much more than a useful metaphor. Geometrically, a perspective representation is exactly equivalent to a tracing of a view on the glass of a window. The artist making the tracing must look with only one eye, fixed at a single point (the eye can revolve, as long as the head remains still). If spectators observed the resulting picture from the same single fixed viewpoint, and with one eye, they would see precisely the same-shaped forms and lines as the artist did when viewing the original scene (although there would, of course, be differences in factors such as colour, distinctness and movement). This is the fundamental principle of conventional, canonical, 'artificial' linear perspective, as it was codified during the Renaissance and continued in eighteenth- and early nineteenth-century British perspective treatises. Throughout this book this mode of representation is referred to as 'standard perspective'.

Standard perspective produces a depiction that appears absolutely accurate when it is viewed from the single correct viewpoint. But if a standard perspective representation is viewed from a point other than the correct one, it can appear distorted and unsatisfactory. This led some artists to question the value of perspective. But the great majority of perspective treatises were concerned only with mathematically accurate perspective and assumed that a picture would be viewed from the single correct viewpoint. One author even suggested: 'I think ... it would be no bad method if our capital landscape painters ... were to write down on the back of the canvas, the height of the centre, and the distance of the perspective plane. For then the picture might be placed to advantage ... [and] would appear to the eye exactly agreeable to the painter's intention.'[7]

In his lectures Turner displayed a great knowledge of standard perspective, and was fully aware of its shortcomings (see Chap.2). He took full account of the practicalities of painting and was at variance with most treatises.[8] He argued that while artists should learn the rules of perspective thoroughly, they should not be shackled by them. This attitude is also evident in his practice, which is examined in Chapter 3.

Professorial Preparations

In spite of his expressed wish to help the 'institution to which I owe everything', Turner seems to have done little work for the lectures in the months following his appointment as professor of perspective. There is no record of any reply from Turner to a letter sent by the Royal Academy Council in December 1808, a year after his election, to enquire whether he 'proposes to lecture this season' (i.e. in early 1809).[9]

However, eventually he set to work in earnest. His official duties were to 'read annually six public lectures ... in which the most useful propositions of geometry, together with the principles of lineal and aerial perspective, shall be fully and clearly illustrated'.[10] Accordingly, he drew up a plan for a course of six lectures, in which, ambitiously, he proposed to include additional subjects, such as 'Backgrounds: Introduction of architecture and landscape', light and shade, and colour. In full, his plan reads:

1. Lecture. Introduction. Its origin, use. How far connected with anatomy, painting, architecture and sculpture. Elements.
   Parallel, angular, aerial perspective.
2. Vision. Subdivision of the elements and forms of perspective.
   Parallel perspective. The cube by the Old Masters.

3. Angular perspective. The circle, [?column]. The difficulties attending the circle. The impropriety of parallel explained.
4. Aerial perspective. Light, shade and colour.
5. Reflexes, reflections and colour.
6. Backgrounds: Introduction of architecture and landscape.[11]

This plan shows that he structured his course with care in an attempt to make his 'arduous … trite, complex [and] indefinite' subject easy for his audience, even if perspective is 'trammelled with the turgid and too often repelling recurrence of mechanical rules'.[12]

Turner made notes from a wide range of sources, some of them apparently far removed from his subject, such as Franciscus Junius, *The Painting of the Ancients* and Pliny the Younger, *Historie of the World*.[13] These historical works may have initially attracted Turner because he was interested in the early development of perspective. This subject pre-occupied him, but was largely unknown to early nineteenth-century Britain. However, he became sidetracked and scribbled down much material relatively marginal to his core subjects. More appropriately, he also consulted a great many perspective treatises. He owned several, and consulted others in the library of the British Museum. His favourite sources were Thomas Malton (Senior), *A Compleat Treatise on Perspective in Theory and Practice on the True Principles of Dr Brook Taylor*, first published in 1775, and John Joshua Kirby's *Dr Brook Taylor's Method of Perspective Made Easy, both in Theory and Practice*, of which he owned a copy of the 1765 third edition. He also consulted at least eight other treatises published in Britain in the eighteenth century, and over a dozen earlier ones in foreign languages.[14] He found some of the latter of minor interest, often copying a solitary diagram, with no accompanying text other than a reference to the author and date of publication.[15]

Turner was adept at extracting information about perspective methods from diagrams. For example, over a period of fifteen years he wrote several descriptions of a method in Guidobaldo del Monte's *Perspectivae* of 1600, basing all his work on a single diagram he had copied into his *Perspective* sketchbook in c.1809. This also provided the source for a large lecture diagram (figs.6–8).[16] In some cases Turner had to rely on diagrams alone because the work concerned was not written in English (although on at least one occasion he seems to have commissioned a translation[17]), but even when he consulted treatises written in English he often paid closer attention to diagrams than text. Clearly diagrams caught his eye as he skimmed through his sources.

The same is true of footnotes: he often ignored the main body of text, preferring to copy supplementary material. He did not read books through from beginning to end. Even those that he valued and con-

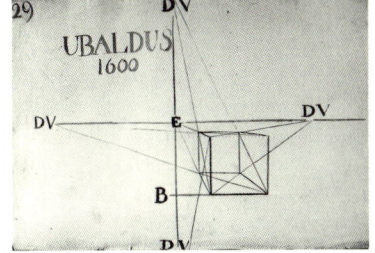

fig.6 'Guidobaldo del Monte's Perspective Method for a Cube', lecture diagram 29 (taken from fig.7) c.1810

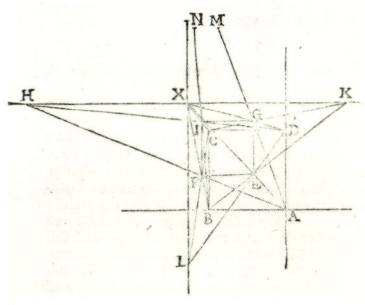

fig.7 Guidobaldo del Monte, *Perspectivae*, 1600, p.135 (detail)

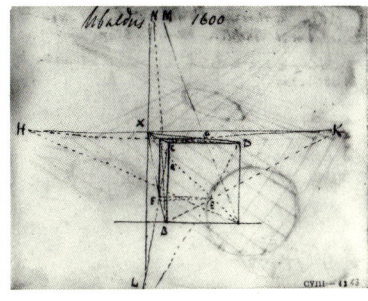

fig.8 *Perspective* sketchbook, Turner's copy of fig.7 c.1809

sulted extensively were not read systematically: his notes reveal that he skipped about, jumping forwards and backwards, jotting down conclusions or peripheral material. This is also clear from the books that he annotated: some pages are heavily marked, but others carry no annotations at all.[18] Turner's somewhat haphazard approach caused him some problems. He made notes on some subjects several times, but completely missed other material of great relevance.[19] If he read some books only partially, he did not read others at all. He had a penchant for quoting 'at second hand': he noted points which his immediate source credited to other authors, then in his lectures attributed them directly to the earlier source, thereby giving the impression (perhaps intentionally) that he had read more widely than was in fact the case.[20]

Occasionally he made errors, sometimes misunderstanding his source so completely that his notes are meaningless.[21] More common, and far more interesting, are those points where a source provided a starting point for his own thoughts. Just as he broke down the work of earlier artists, reassembling it to produce something new, he often adapted the words of others. Sometimes he simply disagreed with his source, and so turned it on its head, or entered into a dialogue with it; but he could also be led off at productive tangents to develop ideas that were quite new. When he agreed with what he read he did not always simply copy it out: sometimes he wrote in his own words, perhaps retaining traces of the original.

Turner's research may have been somewhat unstructured, but it was highly productive and his lectures contain an enormously rich range of material, from a great diversity of sources. However, although many sections of Turner's first drafts for the lectures are of high quality, others amount to little more than direct quotations from books. These passages include material that Turner did not understand, and ideas with which he disagreed. In places he simply listed points worthy of further investigation.

Turner seems to have been well advanced with his first drafts by October 1809, when he informed the Council of the Royal Academy that he would be ready to lecture in the 1810 season.[22] Over the next two months he participated in discussions within the Academy about 'proposed improvements in the lecture room', having particular responsibility for preparing 'designs for lighting the room'.[23] All went well and on 5 January 1810, a matter of weeks before Turner's lecture course was due to begin, the Council 'withdrew to the lecture room, and on their return expressed their satisfaction with the arrangements, preparatory for the lectures, proposed by Messrs Turner and Soane'.[24] By now, Turner had had his own rather untidy first drafts neatly copied, presumably to make them easier to read. All seemed ready.

Then at the Council meeting of 5 February his lectures were postponed. No reasons were given. It could have been because of difficulties in the Academy, but was probably because Turner found that he simply was not ready.[25] He had revised the whole of the first drafts before they were copied, but apparently not extensively enough. Thus the copies he had commissioned were inadequate.

Over the next eleven months he carried out much more work. As soon as the postponement was agreed, he commissioned a further set of copies.[26] He revised these new fine copies extensively and prepared a series of large illustrative diagrams. Finally he was able to lecture; he arranged for a bas relief to be placed in the lecture room, and announcements of the lectures were placed in the newspapers.[27]

At last, Turner's endeavours were ready to be presented to an audience. In January 1811, at the beginning of his first lecture, he explained: 'Alacrity should have appeared earlier in my behalf, but when the continual occurancies and ardours of the profession crowd around, it too often happens that they prevent the completion of greater concerns, and therefore I must wave, saying I am ready that I have pleased myself, or can please.'[28]

Revisions and Repeats

Turner expended great effort and energy to produce his lectures. As shown above, he prepared and revised three separate drafts before the 1811 course. After that, he went on to deliver a course of lectures on at least eleven further occasions between 1812 and 1828.[29] With genuine commitment, he seems to have fully revised his texts each time, often writing entirely new lectures. For example, after delivering the 'Backgrounds' lecture only once in 1811, he seems to have completely replaced it.[30] The extant manuscripts contain over forty separate lecture drafts, and the surviving diagrams and other evidence suggest that there were originally several others.[31] While some manuscripts were quickly abandoned, at least one was in use from the beginning of 1810 until January 1827; it may have been revised as many as ten times.[32]

Most of Turner's drafts (and subsequent copies) were initially written in a single column, taking up only half of each page (fig.1). This left room for Turner's extensive amendments. His approach to revision was often as haphazard as his method of taking notes. He skimmed through his texts, altering or deleting things as they caught his eye, and liberally adding extra passages, working in ink, pencil, and even red paint. He often altered the sequence of pages, sometimes switching them between manuscripts and inserting new pages or scraps of paper which were affixed with adhesive. There may be up to five conflicting series of page numbers in a manuscript. In some cases, the original text can now be distinguished from later additions, enabling it to be studied separately. In others, it is impossible to reconstruct the contents of a manuscript at a specific stage of its development. Occasionally it cannot even be ascertained where different versions of lectures were intended to begin or to end.

The Lecture Diagrams

One of the reasons Turner revised his texts was to relate them more closely to the diagrams that he made to accompany his lectures. Most lectures included between ten and twenty illustrations, many of them large in size. The largest are on Antiquarian sheets; at about 31 by 52 inches, this was the largest paper made by hand in England (figs.21, 22, 36).[33] Many of the lecture diagrams bear large red numbers at their top left-hand corners. There are many corresponding numbers, also in red watercolour, in the lecture texts.

Turner learned a great deal from diagrams and presumably expected his lecture audience to do the same. Indeed, many diagrams are absolutely essential to an understanding of the texts. Some are based on preliminary sketches that Turner made in the lecture drafts, others on ones in his sketchbooks or on loose sheets of paper. He took some images from treatises, but a large number are entirely of his own design. Those based on preliminary sketches in the lecture manuscripts normally relate closely to the text that they accompany, but others are of extremely limited relevance to the lecture passages that they purport to support, as some contemporaries noted: 'Many of his drawings seemed pressed unnecessarily into service and used only as helps to fill in his unhappy pauses.'[34]

However, the lecture illustrations were undoubtedly appreciated by many. For example: 'He elucidated his lecture with some excellent drawings by himself,'[35] and there was talk of 'a well selected series of drawings'.[36] Thomas Stothard, who was virtually deaf, explained that he enjoyed attending Turner's lectures because 'there is much to *see*'.[37]

Ruskin, himself the author of a work on perspective, thought highly of Turner's 'wonderful series of diagrams', which were 'exquisitely tinted, and often completely coloured, all by his own hand, of the most difficult perspective subjects; illustrating not only directions of line, but effects of light, with a care and completion which would put the work of an ordinary teacher to utter shame'.[38]

About one hundred and eighty diagrams are classified as 'Perspective Diagrams' in the inventory of the Turner Bequest. About half of these can be readily associated with the 1811 lecture course, being either diagrams displayed during the lectures, or works preparatory to them. (Many are illustrated in Chapter 2, below.) Others can be associated with later manuscripts, particularly an extended version of the history of perspective techniques,[39] two revisions of material originally contained in lecture 1,[40] later additions to the 1811 version of lecture 3,[41] a series of lectures on geometry, taken directly from Euclid's *Elements* (fig.9),[42] and discussions of colour (fig.10).[43] However, one substantial group of diagrams cannot be matched to any surviving text. They are numbered in sequence from 60 to 76 and include works such as the interiors of prisons and Brocklesby Mausoleum (figs.11–13). A few illustrations from this group are referred to individually, but there is no surviving manuscript that discusses them fully.[44] Some diagrams originally catalogued as illustrations for the perspective lectures are not in fact related to them at all,[45] and others are incomplete.[46] The subjects or sources of most remaining diagrams can be identified, and it may prove possible to relate them to specific texts when further areas of the lecture manuscripts have been studied more fully.[47]

Many of Turner's quick sketches in his lecture texts do not correspond to existing large lecture diagrams, even where they would be extremely relevant. This raises the possibility that many large diagrams have not survived.[48] In addition, Turner illustrated his lectures with works other than large, numbered lecture diagrams. He used his own watercolours, prints after other artists' work, and pieces of sculpture, or at least casts of sculpture. He also regularly referred to Raphael's tapestry cartoons, copies of which were hung in the Great Room of Somerset House, where he lectured (fig.2). He may have drawn diagrams as the lectures progressed.[49] Some diagrams were used to illustrate several completely separate ideas. For example, the watercolour of the 'Temple of Neptune' at Paestum (fig.14 on p.29) is referred to in discussions of: methods for depicting the architectural orders, shadows in oblique sunlight, and the nature of the Doric order.[50] Occasionally diagrams were renumbered, in one case before even the first course of lectures had been given.[51]

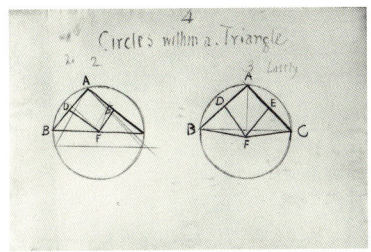

fig.9 'Triangles within Circles', lecture diagram (from *Euclid's Elements of Geometry*, ed. Samuel Cunn, 1759, book 4, proposition 5) c.1817–28

fig.10 'Colour Circle No.1',
lecture diagram c.1822-8

fig.11 'Interior of a Prison',
lecture diagram 65 c.1810

fig.13 'Interior of Brocklesby Mausoleum', lecture diagram 76 c.1810

fig.12 'Interior of a Prison', lecture diagram 66 c.1810

Poor Performance: Adverse Reactions

Unfortunately, Turner did not make the best use of his illustrations. In the words of one critic: 'If Mr Turner would ... personally point out in the drawing the part alluded to in his lectures ... it would probably prove more advantageous to the student than the present mode of displaying them.'[52] Aware of his problems, Turner wrote himself reminders in the margins of his texts: 'call for 60', 'here ends 28', or 'get up 29 – Ubaldus'.[53] He seems to have experimented with alternative modes of presenting the diagrams. In 1819 he was rebuked because the illustrations were too 'hastily placed on and removed from the board'.[54] Consequently, in 1824, he apparently displayed them all for the duration of the lecture, only for a critic to announce that with 'so many figures exposed together', the audience was left 'completely at a loss to know which is referred to, and not infrequently of which particular figure he speaks'. In spite of their not insubstantial size, this latter critic complained that the diagrams illustrating Turner's historical survey of perspective methods were too small. Clearly exasperated, he reported: 'The figures for the most part, and the letters employed in the definition, are in general too small to be clearly perceived at the distance of the seats.'[55]

It was not only in regard to diagrams that Turner's presentational skills stretched the patience of his audience. He not only 'mumbled', but, between his 'unhappy pauses', did so at great speed: in spite of their ambitious scope some of his lectures lasted barely half an hour.[56] There were many reports of his difficulties: 'It is much to be regretted that this highly gifted gentleman, probably from a defect of physical powers, delivered his discourse in such a low tone of voice as to be scarcely audible.'[57] Others were gentler: '[Turner] pointed out ... the best means of acquiring this indispensable branch of knowledge, in a clear if not brilliant mode; and gave a satisfactory course of instruction in a manner not very captivating in its delivery.'[58] Occasionally Turner mislaid diagrams, sometimes even entire lectures. For his first lecture of 1814, he arrived without his portfolio of texts and illustrations. The following week, he began his delayed talk by modestly thanking Henry Fuseli, the professor of painting, who had stepped in to save the evening: 'The loss of my portfolio last Monday, although it caused an interruption of my duty, it created more benefit, I may venture, than the loss of instruction to you, by the able assistance of the professor of painting reading his lecture. Your kindness evinced towards me on that evening ameliorated my embarrassing situation, for which my unfeigned thanks I now offer, together with the hope that you will allow me to particularly thank him for such an act of friendship.'⁵⁹ Turner may have found the whole process of public speaking an embarrassment: some reviews mention his lack of confidence; his 'stammering' and speed as he raced to finish support this assessment as do his humorous self-deprecating remarks about his lecturing abilities.⁶⁰

Many of Turner's lecture texts are overlaid by an extensive series of large red commas. These seem to be substitutes for the more formal punctuation that Turner omitted when he first drafted his texts. A linguistic analysis has shown that these commas are placed at appropriate points, but with alarming frequency. This confirms the view that Turner inserted them in a perhaps frantic attempt to improve his delivery.⁶¹ But the physical state of the lecture manuscripts cannot have helped him: in places they are rendered almost incomprehensible by the weight of amendments they bear. Parts were so heavily re-arranged that it must have been almost impossible for Turner to adhere to the correct sequence. Not only are numerous individual words and paragraphs replaced by others written nearby, but the texts are peppered with symbols such as asterisks, crosses and circles that indicate where he intended to jump from one place to another as he read. There are also instructions such as 'go to the square by Wale' or '24 the Tuscan', 'X Stop Here; go to Pulteney Bridge page 34' or 'Ionic capital 19'. This latter apparently proved to be a particularly troublesome direction to follow, as Turner affixed a little flap of paper, protruding from the rest of the manuscript, to identify the position of the page that he had to locate.⁶² It is easy to imagine Turner being puzzled by the text in front of him. He would start to read, rushing through some passages, hesitating as he attempted to decipher others or follow his directions (fig.15). Furthermore, some of the material that he had noted directly from books, including passages that he did not understand, survived into his 'final' lecture texts. When he read the lectures his confusion would mount: although many parts would be clear and pertinent, others would seem incomprehensible, just as they had years before when he copied them from treatises.

Nevertheless, he received some good press notices, such as 'through the whole of his discourse [Turner] manifested diligent enquiry and accurate knowledge'.⁶³ He was grateful for praise such as this, once writing a long and fulsome poem of thanks to a generous critic.⁶⁴ The amount of detail included in even quite hostile reports shows that many in Turner's audience were perfectly able to understand his remarks, even if not as comfortably as they might have wished. And Turner does not seem to have been the only Royal Academy lecturer whose skills were imperfect: Soane and Fuseli were not immune from abuse, and even Reynolds had often been inaudible.⁶⁵

Turner found lecturing difficult, even painful, and although he

fig.15 John Linnell, 'Study of Turner's Father and Turner's Eyes while Lecturing, 27 January 1812' 1812

lectured fairly regularly during the first twenty years of his office, he completely failed to do so after 1828. Consequently, he suffered further embarrassment and resigned his post after a government inquiry reported on the sorry state of the Royal Academy's lecture programme, particularly the poor performance of its professor of perspective.[66]

Unfortunately, Turner's reputation as an incoherent speaker, together with the confused state of the manuscripts themselves, has led to suggestions that the lectures are worthless. At the beginning of the twentieth century Roger Fry undoubtedly set back the study of them when he advised against publication (for, unlike many other Royal Academy lectures, Turner's had remained unpublished throughout the nineteenth century). Fry wrote: 'I cannot pretend to have read Turner's lectures through ... But I have read considerable parts of them, several almost entirely and I have very little doubt that nothing can be made of them ... What he actually says appears to be almost worthless ... It would be unfair to Turner to publish work which only shows his weaknesses, nor can I imagine that it would have any considerable sale.'[67] Since Fry wrote this, some individuals have made serious attempts to study the lectures,[68] but many others have considered them to be of marginal relevance. With a mixture of Fry's prejudice and utilitarianism, the feeling seemed to be that Turner was not formally educated, so cannot have had many worthwhile things to say; but, in any case, to attempt to find out would not be worth the expenditure of time.

The manuscripts are difficult to study because of the extensive revisions that Turner made to them; and their accessibility is not helped by Turner's appalling handwriting, unusual (or non-existent) punctuation, and confused syntax and phraseology (fig.1). Nevertheless, patient transcription and analysis, together with delicate but thorough editing, renders even apparently opaque texts comprehensible, and shows that Turner could attain a certain elegance in his writing.

In his addresses to the Academy, Turner reached a high level of intellectual sophistication when he dismantled old theories and developed new ones. At the other end of the scale, he conscientiously and comprehensively outlined a vast range of basic perspective techniques for the benefit of his audience. Although linear perspective dominates the lectures (as it should), other topics await the diligent scholar. There are the experiments into optics of lecture 5 (figs.50–3); discussions of pictorial composition, the depiction of ancient architecture (fig.14), and the structure of the eye; and numerous accounts of the relationships between painting and poetry, of light and shade, and of the role and nature of colour (fig.10), to list but a selection. Perhaps surprisingly, there is virtually nothing about aerial perspective; but the manuscripts do include around half a dozen different versions of what was lecture 1 in 1811, and there is much additional perspectival and geometrical material.

An analysis of those sections that concern linear perspective (summarised below in Chapter 2) shows that Turner's lectures contain a wealth of intelligent, sophisticated discussion of art and its problems and can offer many insights into his practice as a painter. That the same is true of other parts of the manuscripts is suggested by the work of those scholars who have made tentative use of them over the past thirty years. No serious studies of Turner's art can hope to be complete without taking account of material in his lectures: it is time to recognise the central position that they occupy in his work.

fig.14 'The "Temple of Neptune" at Paestum', lecture diagram c.1810

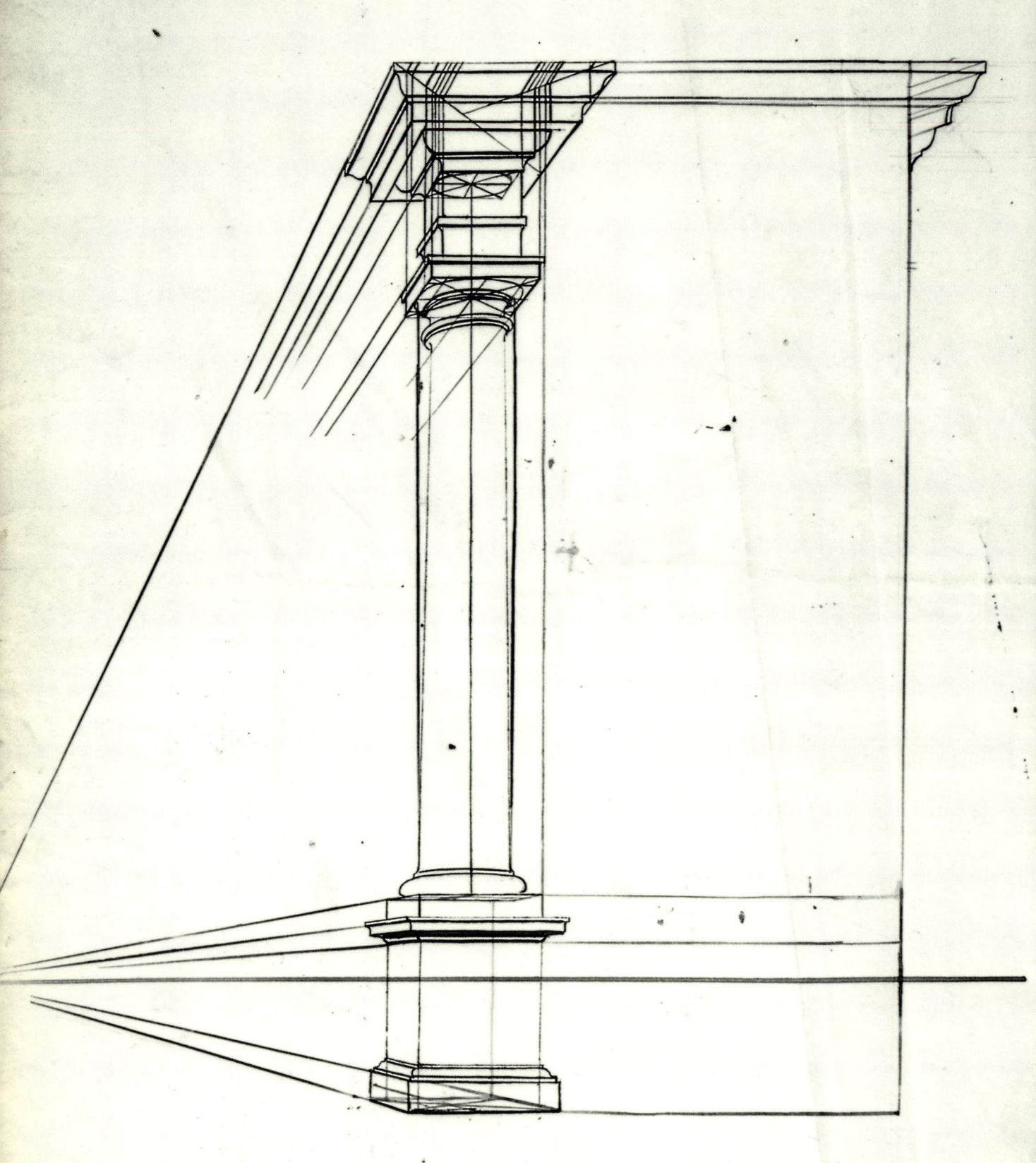

CHAPTER 2 TURNER'S 1811 LECTURES

Lecture 1: The Importance of Perspective and Geometry

'Lines of Praise'

Turner began his long-awaited first perspective lecture at 8pm on Monday 7 January 1811, before 'the President [Benjamin West], many of the members, and a considerable number of auditors,' according to a review in the following day's edition of the *Sun*. The reviewer characterised the lecture as 'rather introductory than technical, and principally intended to show that the highest order of historical painters, as well as architects and sculptors, availed themselves of the principles of perspective in their most distinguished productions.'[1] This assessment coincides with Turner's own detailed plan for the first lecture. After an introduction and the 'elogium upon Sir Joshua', the plan continues with: 'Rise of perspective. Its use connected with anatomy; painting; sculpture of ancients – where made use of and neglected; architecture – geometric rules and drawings, where improper. Perspective of importance to proportion and design, exemplified in the "Transfiguration". Settled.'[2]

This syllabus shows that in his first lecture Turner aimed to link perspective with all the four other fields in which the Royal Academy offered professorships: anatomy, sculpture, architecture and painting. This seems an eccentric undertaking, but it offered ample opportunity to demonstrate the importance of Turner's subject. However, it presupposed the adoption of an extremely catholic conception of 'perspective', much wider than linear perspective itself. The lecture is mainly about the way in which geometry enters into art. For example, Turner's discussion of 'perspective' and anatomy was almost solely concerned with the way in which basic shapes, such as triangles, can be found in the human body; in support of this he cited the anatomical work of Leonardo 'in the possession of His Majesty'[3] and Michelangelo's rule, given to a pupil, that 'he should always make a figure pyramidal or serpentlike by multiplying two and three'.[4] At this point Turner displayed his own diagram of Raphael's 'Transfiguration' (fig.23)[5] and two diagrams for which he gave the source as 'Albert Dürer'. He explained that one of these (fig.16) 'is a plan of a figure

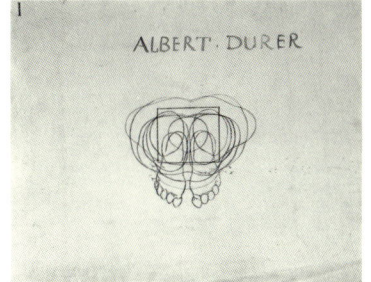

fig.16 'Cross-sections of the Human Body', lecture diagram 1 (after Dürer) c.1810

'Perspective Construction of a Tuscan Column', lecture diagram 41 c.1810 (detail of fig.45)

viewed at the feet horizontally. Each circle is that which a horizontal section would produce at different well known heights.'⁶

Turner's comments about sculpture also had little to do with perspective in a strict sense. He stressed the need to take due account of the height at which a sculpture was intended to be displayed, and to proportion it accordingly. He gave several examples from ancient history and from contemporary London: he drew on Junius's *Painting of the Ancients* to give a long account of the attempts of Phidias and Alcamenes to make statues of Minerva;⁷ he entered the controversy as to whether the spiral bas relief on Trajan's column becomes larger as it rises (fig.17); he discussed the appearance of the 'flaming ball' at the top of the Monument (fig.18), based on observations he had made about the distance one must be from its base in order to be able to see it fully (fig.19);⁸ and he considered the appearance of the statue of George I that surmounts the steeple of St George's, Bloomsbury (figs.20, 92).⁹

Next came the perspective of bas reliefs and a highly irrelevant digression about the artistic powers of the Carracci. This was followed by architecture. Here, Turner was able to link his subject to linear perspective proper, because he concentrated on architectural drawing.

fig.17 'Trajan's Column', lecture diagram 5 *c*.1810

fig.18 'The Monument', lecture diagram 4 *c*.1810

He argued that architects should prepare perspective views of buildings because geometrical elevations are not always suitable. The latter 'may point out the size and scale of buildings, but ... the relative proportions of each design becomes exclusively the province of perspective delineation to explain, by exemplifying the parts under various angles, in the same way as they would be seen in nature.'[10] Elevations of ancient temples can fail to reveal the number of columns and whether they are freestanding or not.[11] However, 'with the aid of perspective their distinction commences, the proportion and ordinance of each style becomes defined, accompanied by an appearance of altitude, of nature and of truth.'[12] Perhaps the worst possible approach is to shade a geometrical elevation, using 'aerial perspective' to 'graduat[e] tones of distance'. For, 'if perspective is improper in the first instance, her appearance in any part of geometric compositions becomes highly improper. Measures [i.e. measurements to scale] and measures only are the things required, and should be looked for in elevations; but they cease to be measures of parts, upon a pictorial effect being even attempted.'[13]

To demonstrate, Turner displayed two illustrations of buildings behind screens of columns. One shows Carlton House (fig.21); designed by Henry Holland, built 1783–95, demolished 1826) in geometrical elevation, but shaded – partly to take account of the distance between the main building and the screen. Turner complained about the incongruous aesthetic effect of such shaded elevations and warned that they mislead by giving a false impression of the appearance of the finished building: 'light, shadow or colour adds a kind of quality to [geometrical elevations] that may appear to some like truth, and lead others to suppose that any building happily proportioned geometric must appear so when executed, and those parts which seem to rise higher by the aid of a lighter tone will appear as lofty when built. No, but quite the reverse: the expanded, massy and towering dome that always appears ready to crush the supporting portico in geometrical drawings would, [as] it were, sink; and then would sink perhaps the character of the whole fabric by its insignificance.'[14]

Turner felt that his other illustration, of the Admiralty on Whitehall (fig.22; designed 1722–6 by Thomas Ripley, with the screen of 1758 Robert Adam's first major work), was more acceptable, as the main building is in perspective and so better represents its actual appearance. However, there was an inconsistency, with the screen 'being square in all places to the eye', but the main building reduced with 'obliquity, gradation and diminution, the features of perspective'.[15] Thus, neither illustration was offered as an appropriate model. The important thing was for architects to have an adequate knowledge of perspective: 'Consequently perspective becomes an essential part of the

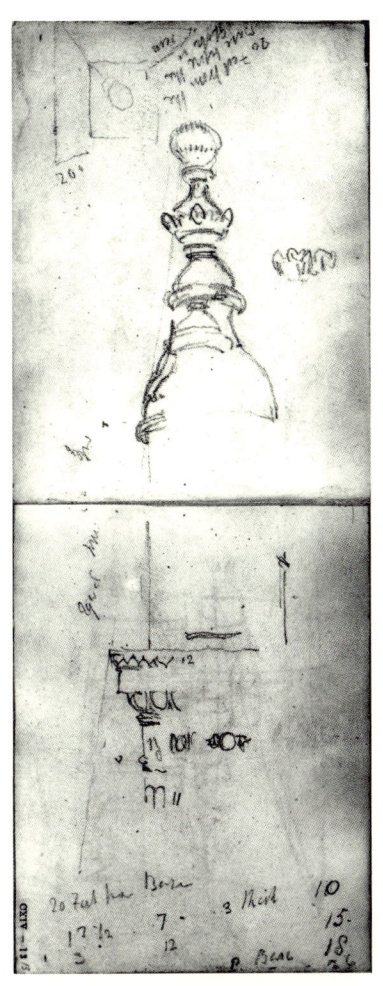

fig.19 *Windmill and Lock* sketchbook, Notes about viewing the Monument *c*.1809

student's studies in architecture, that he may not only make use of its rules to assist his designs, but to know what those designs properly would look and may be if put into practice.'[16]

As in the rest of the first lecture, Turner's theme was the importance of perspective and geometry when he considered painting. Towards the beginning of the lecture he presented some key events from the early history of perspective, beginning with the ancients. He aimed to demonstrate: 'Mechanical rules assume completely the guidance of our path, and it requires something to encourage us on our way … A steady attention to those who have preceded us in the same pursuit will be highly necessary to obtain at least some proficiency for ourselves by the same rules. And as the greatest masters of antiquity have left us manifold proofs of their value of geometry, it cannot be arrogating to infer that perspective enters into the primary order of painting: namely drawing.'[17] After a few concise examples, he moved swiftly on, noting that Dürer was normally credited with 'adducing the art to some fixed method or rules of geometric proportions … yet it cannot be inferred that all the painters prior to that period … to have been so deficient of vision as to be blind to the obliquity of lines'.[18] Turner determined to give credit to those whose 'discoveries probably furnished the means to … Dürer'[19] and mentioned several earlier artists, including Cimabue, Jan van Eyck, Stephano Florentino and Paolo Uccello, but made no mention here of Alberti or Brunelleschi.[20] His key point was: 'The earliest attention of the restorers of modern art [i.e. artists of the early Renaissance] to [perspective] rules is sufficient to establish the necessity of their introduction into the first class of painting, namely that of invention. Not into the most creative, indescribable and inscrutable cause which receives, gives, or produces

fig.20 'St.George's, Bloomsbury', lecture diagram 6 c.1810

fig.21 'Carlton House', lecture diagram c.1810

the idea – at once the noblest and, of course, the highest part of art – but immediately into the immediate practice, application and imitation of such ideas, however excited or created, by giving them a pictorial local situation ... and to each its form, light, shadow, position and gradation.'[21]

This material on the early history of perspective in fact preceded that on anatomy. To link the two discussions Turner quoted Algarotti to the effect that 'a picture designed according to the rules of perspective and the principles of anatomy will ever be held higher in esteem by good judges than a picture ill drawn, let it be ever so well coloured. For nature, though she forms men of various colours and complexions, never operates upon their motions contrary to the mechanical principles of anatomy, nor in exhibiting those motions to the eye against the geometrical laws of perspective.'[22]

Turner returned to this theme towards the end of the lecture. With strong echoes of Reynolds's insistence on the importance of study, he demanded that young artists followed rules and did not rely on 'genius'.[23] Linear perspective forms a large part of the rules that artists must learn: 'Although for the sake of avoiding a little trouble it has often been advanced that the study of perspective is a drudgery and a toil, while the observation of nature is pleasant all, and which must be admitted; but we are not always so happily placed as to be able to

fig.22 'The Admiralty', lecture diagram 10 (see also fig.23) c.1810

consult her unerring laws or study her effects. Our observations may not have been sufficient retained, or perhaps defective, we may be required to change our point and our light and shade, and then the consequences, the inefficiency, of relying wholly upon observation perplexes and stamps conviction of the necessity of a thorough knowledge of rules to avoid absurdity ... The hand drawing only from the impulse of observation on the mind ... often commits blunders as to rules. When the impetuousity of genius travels on without a guide, it too often finds itself in doubt about ... the obliquity of a line. To these rules perspective lies an undivided claim. In composition and invention she follows to correct, but those acquainted with her laws and nature will design perspectively.'[24] Note that at the end of this passage Turner implied that rules alone are not enough, but artists must take account of both 'laws and nature' – a theme he developed in subsequent lectures.

fig.23 'The Proportion and Design of Raphael's "Transfiguration"', lecture diagram 10 (see also fig.22) c.1810

Here, he concluded with an examination of the work of Raphael. He praised the 'proportion and design' of the 'Transfiguration', offering a rather contrived analysis of the geometry that underlies its composition (fig.23).[25] He then considered the importance of Raphael's subtle use of perspective in his tapestry cartoons (figs.2, 54). Turner felt this had not adequately been recognised: 'The lights and shadows have received their share of praise, and even the different-toned colours of the garments ... but the lines ... as lines have never had a line of praise, because they are thought fetters to genius.'[26]

Lecture 2: Standard Perspective and its Problems

'Circuitously Cautious for a Painter's Pursuit'

Turner began his second lecture by dismissing as irrelevant debate about the process of vision and the operation of the eye. As far as standard linear perspective is concerned, the important thing is simply that 'forms, however they are conveyed to the mind ... should be distinctly delineated upon a plane surface, as to be allowed to express particularly each object and its angles as they appear to the eye'.[27] He explained that standard perspective rests upon the assumption that 'the boundary lines of each figure gives itself in right lines [i.e. light travels in straight lines – a basic property he questioned elsewhere in his lectures[28]], and therefore makes a cone of visual rays'.[29] He illustrated this model of vision, with the eye at the apex of a cone of rays of light

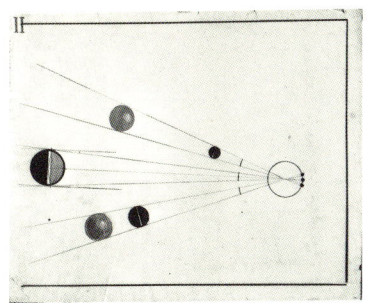

fig.24 'Spheres at Different Distances from the Eye', lecture diagram 11 (after Thomas Malton, *A Compleat Treatise on Perspective*, 1775, pl.1, fig.3) c.1810

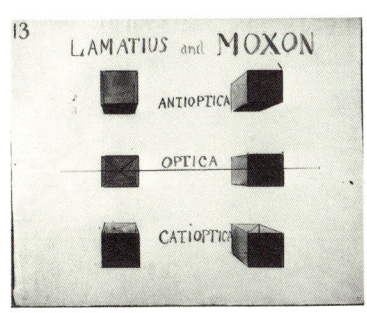

fig.25 'Objects Above, Level with, and Below the Eye', lecture diagram 13 (after Giovanni Paolo Lomazzo, *A Tracte Containing the Artes of Curious Paintinge, Carvinge and Buildinge*, English trans. R. Haydocke, Oxford 1598, p.204) c.1810

travelling from objects, in a diagram (fig.24), simplified from one in Thomas Malton's *Compleat Treatise*. Turner continued: 'all objects appear in proportion to their several angles under which they are seen … Supposing three globes at different distances: if the first be half the distance of the second one to the eye, [and] the third twice the distance of the second, [then] the angles they subtend at the eye – if the diameters are in proportion to their distances – will be equal; consequently they are to the eye equal.'[30] At the right of the diagram all the spheres have the same size image on the retina of the eye.

Turner next paraphrased a footnote to Malton's text, to explain that when a sphere is viewed, 'the exact diameter … cannot be seen, because of the convergency of the visual rays'.[31] In the illustration, the lighter strip across each sphere represents the difference between the full diameter of the sphere and what the eye perceives that diameter to be. This subject fascinated Turner as it suggested that there was a fundamental difference between vision and perspective; he returned to it later in the lecture, with a further diagram to illustrate it (fig.31). Here, he outlined and illustrated some further basic phenomena of vision, such as 'parallel right lines appear to approach each other and meet in a point in an infinite distance' and 'a … horizontal surface below the eye appears to rise, and one above the horizontal line [i.e. horizon] to incline [downwards], that each of the lines would … meet in a point on the horizon' (fig.25).[32] Turner noted that perspective treatises explained a standard perspective representation as a vertical plane intersecting the cone of vision (figs.3, 4), as illustrated in 'the famed fenestre of Albert Dürer', which he had earlier copied into his *Perspective* sketchbook (fig.5). But Turner was unimpressed by the concept: 'Simplicity is its only beauty and when divested of its intricacies with which … it has been clothed is nothing more than a supposed plane between the eye and the object on which that object is supposed to strike in its passage by right lines.'[33]

After this, Turner gave verbatim some of Malton's definitions of perspective terminology and paraphrased others; he also added comments and definitions of his own, devoting several pages of his lecture draft and three diagrams (which he attributed to Moxon, Brook Taylor and Thomas Malton Junior) to the subject (figs.26–8). However, Turner's definitions were often inadequate, or even inaccurate. Together with a selection of axioms from Euclid's *Elements* (via Malton) that followed them, the definitions were not presented with clarity; some were so severely curtailed that they made little sense. Furthermore the definitions in lecture 2 bore little relation to the terminology Turner was to employ when he presented practical techniques of perspective in lectures 3 and 4. There, he prided himself on his ability to avoid what he felt to be unnecessary jargon.[34]

Turner's brevity suggests that he did not care for the theoretical approach of eighteenth- and early nineteenth-century treatises. This attitude can also be identified in his attack on the approach to perspective of the mathematician Brook Taylor. Taylor had revolutionised the study of standard perspective in publications of 1715 and 1719 and was highly praised by almost all eighteenth-century British perspective writers. Malton explained that Taylor was unable 'to convey the ideas he intended to inculcate by the old terms, and therefore was under the necessity of inventing and enforcing new ones',[35] but Turner disagreed, arguing 'whether ... his ideas ... could not be conveyed by the old terms may be doubted' and noting, with despair: 'Alas, he has left us much tautology.'[36] Perspective was approached as an almost abstract theory by writers such as Taylor. Malton agreed with this approach: 'The position [of] the horizon is not considered at all; as the theorems are general and applicable in all positions of the picture whatever; since (as Dr Brook Taylor in his preface to his second treatise justly observes) all planes, simply as planes, are alike in geometry.'[37] In the first draft of his second lecture Turner began to copy this passage, but stopped abruptly in mid-sentence, deleted part of what he had just written and, almost in reply to the attitudes of Taylor and Malton, protested: 'It must be extremely difficult to define what we are to consider.' His patience had worn thin and he exclaimed that while the approach of treatises may be 'a useful and a well beaten road to science', it is 'circuitously cautious for a painter's pursuit'.[38] Turner required only straightforward 'rules' that would work for artists in practice. He did not see any need to build perspective up on a theoretical foundation of Euclidian geometry. In his lectures he proved no theorems and did not rigorously justify his recommended techniques. But he warned that his practical approach did not mean that students could avoid study: 'The shortest way to perspective is through theory to practice; the loss of time (if any) will never be regretted.'[39]

Turner next moved into an area that fascinated him: the ability of the system of standard perspective to cope with curved objects; he called this subject 'curvilinear perspective' (a term that is used quite differently in the twentieth century[40]). In *The Art of Painting*, Du Fresnoy had argued: 'Yet deem not, youths, that perspective can give/ those charms complete by which your works shall live ... the true genius scorns her rigid laws/ By nature taught he [*sic*] strikes th'unerring lines,/ Consults his eye, and as he sees designs.'[41] Turner disagreed and insisted that Du Fresnoy was expending 'spleen ... upon an art [later altered to 'science' and then to 'theory'!] which he never truly appreciated. [To] accompany study, not to dictate; to improve or to remove imperfection; to guide, not control; is the object of perspective. But he allows it not to be a guide, but conceiving it to control and shackle all

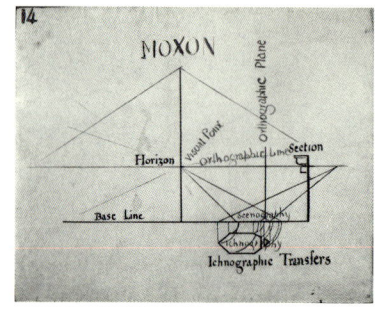

fig.26 'The Terminology of Perspective of Joseph Moxon', lecture diagram 14 *c.*1810

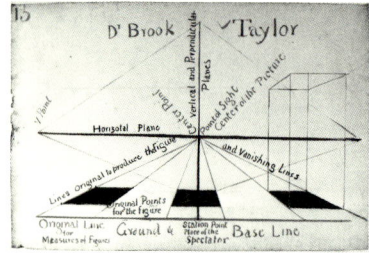

fig.27 'The Terminology of Perspective of Brook Taylor', lecture diagram 15 *c.*1810

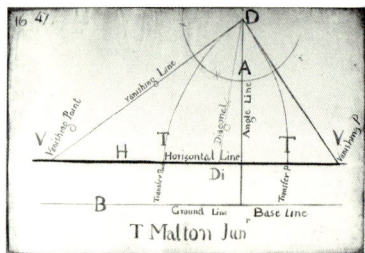

fig.28 'The Terminology of Perspective of Thomas Malton Junior', lecture diagram 16, later renumbered 47 *c.*1810

fig.29 'Conic and Cylindrical Sections', lecture diagram 19 (after Thomas Malton, *A Compleat Treatise on Perspective*, 1775, figs.27–9, pl.7) *c*.1810

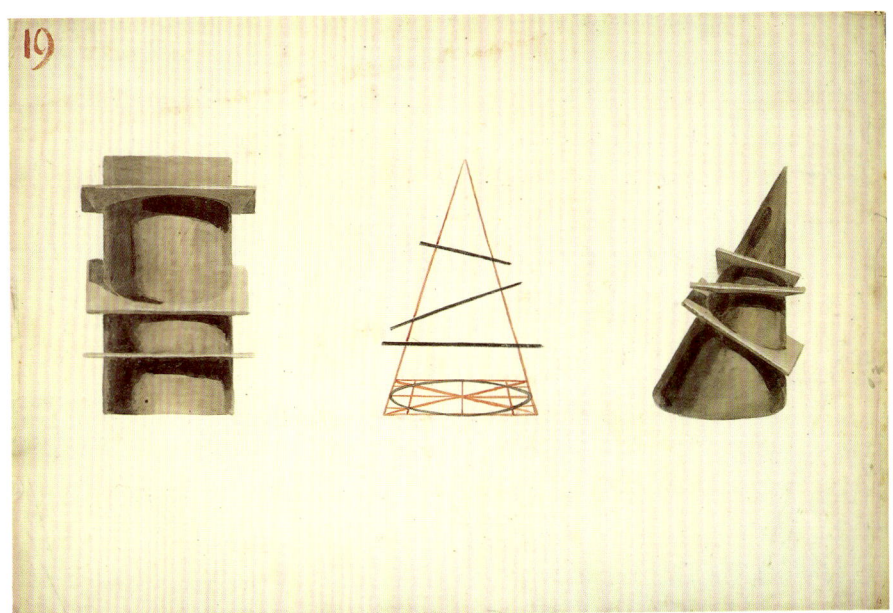

fig.30 'The Geometry of a Parabola', lecture diagram 23 (after John Hamilton, *Stereography*, 1738, fig.84, no.1) *c*.1810

idea, he wished to leave everything to the perceptions of genius ... let us hope ... that his practice was not guided by such a theory.'[42] Turner observed with satisfaction that Sir Joshua Reynolds, in his notes on the passage, also saw the need for perspective regulation: 'His able annotator [Reynolds] ... would have deprived us of more knowledge than the originator [Du Fresnoy] on this point, had he withheld his high sense of the propriety of confiding and conforming the fertility of invention to rules, which will inevitably lead you, says Sir Joshua, the shortest way to excellence.'[43] Turner stressed that even curved objects that seem beyond 'the power or rules' of perspective, will be depicted better by artists who have a good knowledge of the subject: 'The various branches of study: history, portrait and landscape – indeed, every class of painting – often require their [i.e. the rules of perspective's] cooperation, and have often proved their usefulness and the dire necessity of knowing [rules] early ... by [the] impropriety which arises from neglecting them.'[44]

Next, Turner presented a straightforward account of the role of conic sections in the geometry of perspective. Like much material earlier in lecture 2, it is based mainly on Malton, as are some of the accompanying diagrams (e.g. fig.29), although Turner did augment the account with other material, including two diagrams which have their origins in sketches that he made from John Hamilton's *Stereography* of 1738, even though he attributed one of them to 'Emmerson' (fig.30).[45]

Of more interest to Turner was a footnote to Malton's discussion of conic sections. The note refers the reader back to the discussion of 'apparent diameters' of spheres. Although Turner had already discussed this phenomenon at the beginning of the lecture, he returned to it and also prepared a further lecture diagram illustrating it (fig.31).[46] This diagram shows the rays from three spheres to the eye. In the central one the black line represents its 'true diameter', while the paler (red) one represents the apparent diameter that the viewer of the sphere would perceive. Malton did not discuss the difference between the two diameters in much more detail, but Turner was evidently intrigued by it. He made several further points, particularly about the importance of distinguishing between circles and squares when choosing methods of perspective. He argued that cubes and squares do not behave in the same way as spheres and circles, because the eye is able to see the full width of a cube. Elsewhere in the lectures Turner drew his audience's attention to the fact that in spite of this difference, many treatises recommended depicting circles by first drawing squares around them. He felt that this practice gave an awkward appearance to the circles so produced: 'The inclined appearance a circle assumes when produced by the square … (the usual way to find circles) every practitioner must be well aware of … convincing that some radical defect exists somewhere in rules.'[47] There are more layers to Turner's argument, but it is clear that, in this area at least, he felt standard perspective to be fundamentally flawed.

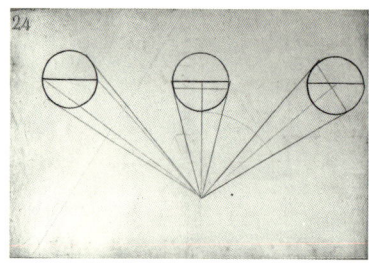

fig.31 'Real and Apparent Diameters of Spheres', lecture diagram 24 c.1810

Turner continued lecture 2 by making further objections to standard perspective. To illustrate a difficulty now known as 'marginal distortion', he presented the three column problem. In this classic problem (which was considered first by Leonardo) perspective is used to depict a row of (three or more) columns parallel to the picture plane and quite close to it – an arrangement that would occur if an artist were depicting the view from within a portico or looking straight across the nave of a church from within an aisle (fig.32). In the resulting picture it is found, somewhat surprisingly, that the column furthest from the artist has the widest representation on the picture surface (fig.33). To a subsequent viewer at the single correct viewpoint, standard perspective representations appear exactly the same shape and size as the original objects did to the artist who made the representation; thus, the increase in size of the representations of the columns is not evident. However, to spectators at other viewpoints the representations of the columns can appear larger, thereby causing the margins of the picture to seem distorted – hence the term 'marginal distortion' (fig.34).

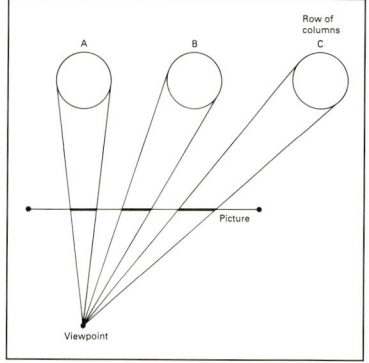

fig.32 Plan of the arrangement of the three column problem (modern diagram)

Turner's main examination of this problem began with material taken from his own copy of a 1710 English translation of Bernard Lamy's treatise. He reported Lamy's view that standard perspective was incorrect in its assumption that the perceived size of an object is related only to the angle it subtended at the eye: '[According to Lamy] there is a natural kind of trigonometry in vision that proportionates

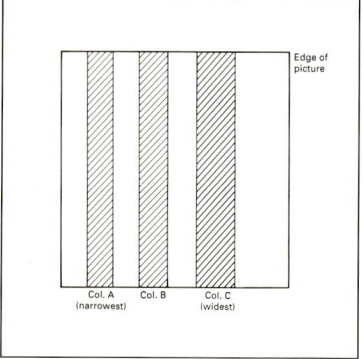

fig.33 The representation produced by the arrangement in fig.32 (modern diagram)

and determines the situation of every object. [He] censures [the] axiom that what is seen under the same angle appears equal, which according to him is capable of making us commit great mistakes in the practice.'[48] Lamy's discussion of the three column problem came much later in the treatise. To illustrate it, Turner produced two large lecture diagrams (figs.35–6); these bear some relationship to ones Lamy used, but were mainly of Turner's own design.[49] First, Turner considered the problem of depicting a row of 'pilasters' (in fact, square-shaped pillars) that was parallel to the picture plane. He found that the standard perspective representations of the front faces of the pilasters were all the same size, and the representations of the side faces became larger as they got further from the viewpoint. Thus, the overall width of each representation increased, as Turner indicated by the thick horizontal lines in figure 35. Once the square bases of the pilasters were put into perspective, it would then be easy to complete the depiction by raising the sides of the pilasters on their corners.

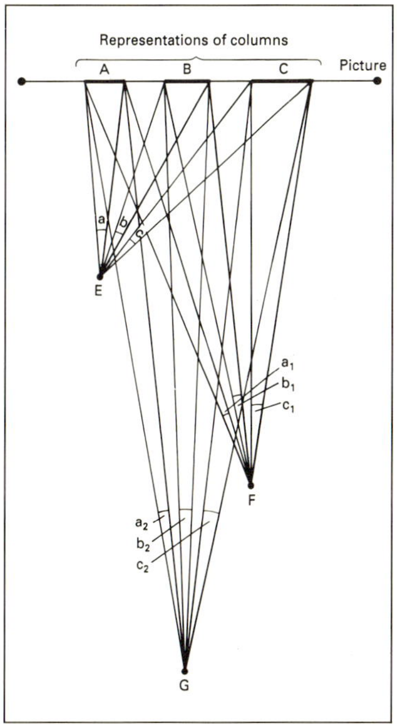

However, if round columns were substituted for the square-shaped pillars, a complication would arise: a column has a circular base; not only is it difficult to put this into perspective in the first place, but there are no corners to the base on which to raise the sides representing the edges of the part of the column that can be seen. Turner summarised Lamy's point: 'But the difficulty is what points of these bases we should raise perpendicular to enclose the visible part of the columns.'[50] The difficulty is alluded to at the far right of one of Turner's lecture diagrams (fig.36).

Lamy concluded his account of the problem by observing that to have the representations of the columns increasing in width 'cannot be sensible'. Turner agreed with this point and then looked at the coverage of marginal distortion in other treatises. He began with Kirby, whose ideas he presented very briefly, without fully appreciating their significance.[51] Kirby had argued that the results of standard perspective should be ignored and all the columns should be represented the same width. This suggestion had caused outrage, and Kirby was attacked by many writers on perspective, including Joseph Highmore, Edward Noble and Thomas Malton. Malton stressed that there is a fundamental difference between the perspective representation of an object and its 'appearance': 'The cause of all [Kirby's and others'] false notions in perspective is their not rightly distinguishing between the representation of an object on a plane and the true appearance of it; two distinct things which can never be united on a plane surface of a picture.'[52] This distinction is crucial. With its single viewpoint, standard perspective is quite different to the experience of vision. Theorists like Malton were concerned only with mathematically accurate perspective and assumed that a picture would be viewed from the single correct

fig.34 The effect of viewing fig.33 from different viewpoints.

From the correct viewpoint, E, angle a is larger than angle b, which is larger than angle c, so column A appears the largest and column C the smallest as would be expected because column A was closest to the artist.

However, from other viewpoints the columns can appear incorrect. For example, from F: angle c_1 is larger than angles a_1 or b_1, so column C appears the largest. Similarly, from G: c_2 is larger than a_2 or b_2, so column C appears the largest.

This shows that a standard perspective construction can appear distorted if viewed from points other than the single fixed viewpoint.

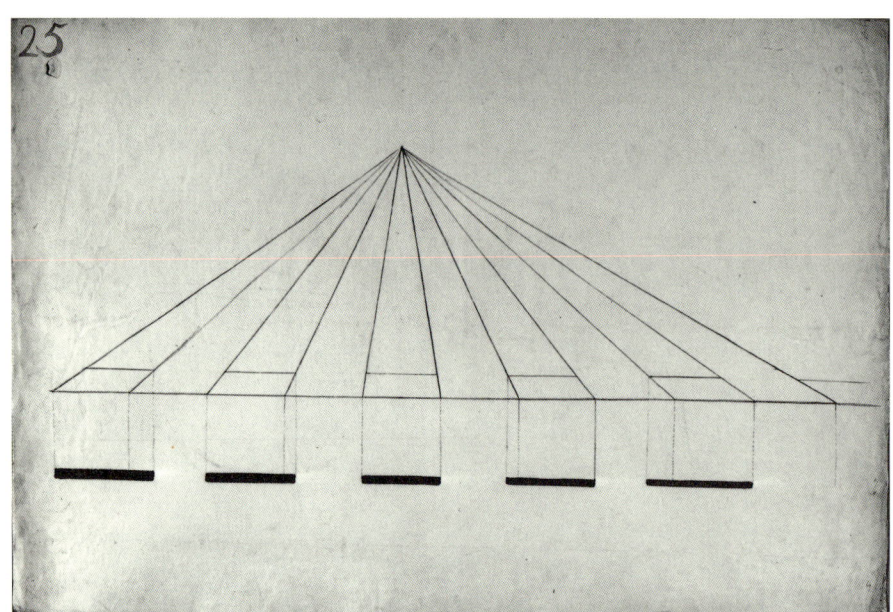

fig.35 'Analysis of the Perspective Representation of a Row of Pillars Parallel and Close to the Picture Plane', lecture diagram 25 c.1810

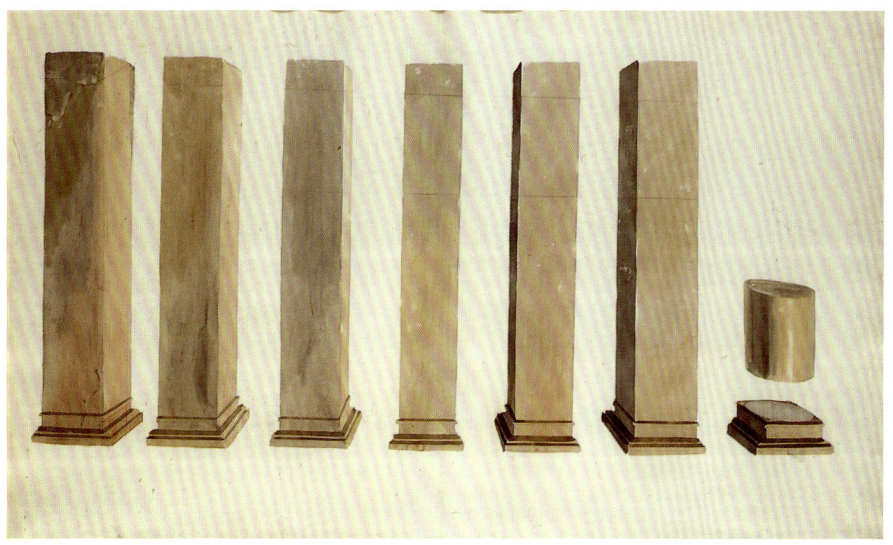

fig.36 'Perspective Representation of a Row of Pillars and a Column Parallel and Close to the Picture Plane', lecture diagram c.1810

viewpoint. If it was not, the fault was with the viewer and not with perspective.

Like Kirby, Turner was unconvinced by the unfailing belief in standard perspective's validity held by the great majority of writers on perspective. Turner observed that in spite of their high ideals, many authors did concede that standard perspective fared badly when short viewing distances were adopted, and so recommended that in practice artists avoided them. These recommendations were usually expressed in terms of the maximum permissible angle of view, with a short distance being equivalent to a large angle.[53] But Turner was completely unwilling to accept 'any such trammel upon painting' and exploded: 'But as painters we have to do with perspective in those very distortions.' He parodied a conversation that Rubens would have had to have had, had he adhered to this constraint: 'Would he have said "my picture is painted for a certain angle to view it", or, "I cannot introduce that thing because it is within the angle of 45°"? No! His works tell us what he thought and what he dared to do.'[54]

Turner attacked further aspects of standard perspective, and showed one further diagram (fig.94). He then concluded the second lecture with an assessment of the value of perspective rules rather more measured than that which ended his previous lecture. Now, having made his audience aware that some aspects of perspective were flawed, he demanded that there should be a 'joint coincidence'[55] between rules and nature: 'Rules are the means, nature the end.'[56] However, the conflict between perspective rules and 'natural' vision still does not mean that artists could simply abandon rules, 'on the contrary, [the deviation] should impel us onwards, not by prejudice for or against any one system, or perniciously adhering to, and condemning all practice by, contradictions ... but by knowing how far [rules] are valuable. Then the knowledge of rules begins to create a confidence unattainable by any other method, which conjunctively with our reasoning faculties, enables the mind not only to act for itself, but to duly appreciate with truth and force what nature's laws declare.'[57]

Lectures 3 and 4: Practical Perspective Techniques

'The Mechanical Excellence of Rules'

After demonstrating the value of perspective in his first lecture, and discussing aspects of its underlying theory in the second, Turner presented methods of practical perspective in lectures 3 and 4. His plan for the lectures shows that he originally intended to begin with the relatively simple techniques of 'parallel' perspective – which can be used only for rectangular objects with one face parallel to the picture plane. These were to be followed by more widely applicable, but more complex and difficult, methods of 'angular' perspective. Turner distinguished between the two (both categories of standard perspective): 'Parallel perspective ... as an aid to the student is of considerable import by facilitating the knowledge of the rules generally by evading in the first instance the seeming perplexity arising from the double points and transfer lines of angular perspective.'⁵⁸ He had doubts about the theoretical validity of parallel perspective (additional to his worries about standard perspective as a whole), but still felt it to be of great value to artists and explained how 'the early masters', particularly Dürer and Raphael, 'made great use of it'.⁵⁹ He attempted to determine the date at which techniques of angular perspective had been first devised, but was unable to reach a conclusion.⁶⁰

Turner continued by presenting methods for depicting cubes in perspective, selected from a wide range of perspective treatises, dating from 1505 to 1700. This presentation developed out of an extensive programme of research for which he studied almost twenty different historical methods of perspective. His research was wider in scope than anything that had been published on the history of perspective and may represent the most ambitious study of the subject undertaken before the middle of the nineteenth century.⁶¹ He researched most methods directly from original treatises; although he took details of some from Kirby's small selection of historical methods.⁶² In 1811 Turner probably presented nine different methods in detail, most of which were illustrated in large lecture diagrams (e.g. figs.6, 37–8), and mentioned several others.⁶³ He became interested in such a wide variety of perspective techniques that he encompassed methods of both parallel and angular perspective, some of them quite complicated. In doing so, he defeated his aim of introducing perspective methods as painlessly as possible by presenting only simple ones of parallel perspective first.

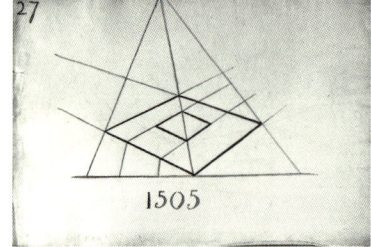

fig.37 'Perspective Method for a Square' (attributed by Turner to Viator (Jean Pelerin)), lecture diagram 27 c.1810

Next came techniques of angular perspective. Turner stressed its relevance: 'In angular perspective we must not consider [exercises] as diagrams, but as positive pieces of nature … every cube and circle is convertible into a building by subdivisions or addition.'⁶⁴ Using a method that includes a plan of the object, he first depicted a simple rectangular shape in perspective (fig.39) and then developed it into a house by the addition of basic architectural features – a door with steps, windows, a pediment, and a cornice (fig.40). In a further diagram he demonstrated that such a perspective construction can be used to produce an elegant watercolour (fig.41).

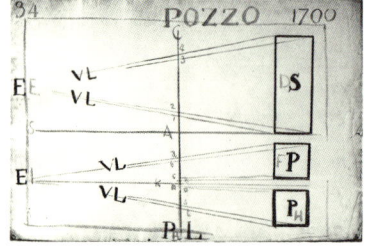

fig.38 'Perspective Method by Andrea Pozzo', lecture diagram 34 (taken from John Joshua Kirby, *Dr Brook Taylor's Method of Perspective Made Easy*, 1768, book 2, pl.19, fig.6) c.1810

However, Turner's method was not entirely accurate as the vanishing points were incorrectly positioned.⁶⁵ A basic characteristic of standard perspective is that all representations of lines that are parallel to each other meet at a single point, known as their vanishing point. (If the lines are horizontal, then this vanishing point will be on the horizon.) A fundamental step in any perspective construction is that of locating the vanishing points; if they are wrongly positioned then objects will inevitably be depicted incorrectly. A comparison of Turner's diagram of a house to a correct construction reveals a substantial difference (fig.42). But errors in the lecture diagrams have not been widely noted: they are only apparent after careful analysis. Indeed, Turner's lecture diagrams, and most of his other pictures, demonstrate that strictly accurate perspective is not essential to a successful work of art. Perspective precision is much more a matter of mathematical, rather than artistic, interest. Nevertheless, in terms of the teaching of perspective, Turner's error is so fundamental that it is scarcely credible that he made it. Every treatise that Turner consulted for full techniques of angular perspective gave vanishing points correctly. It is even more surprising when his extensive experience of perspective is taken into account. Even in the same diagram he correctly used a number of sophisticated and subtle techniques; for example, to depict the triangular pediment that forms the eaves of the roof.

Turner's error should not be taken as an indication that his knowledge of perspective was poor, rather it supports the conclusion that he was not interested in absolute theoretical and geometrical accuracy. His accounts of perspective procedures are brief in comparison to ones in eighteenth- and early nineteenth-century perspective treatises, where very specific problems and the exact relationships between artist, picture and object are precisely stated. Turner tended to outline the key characteristics of a technique in rather broad terms, often omitting details such as how to locate the vanishing points, what the different lines and points used in constructions represent, or how measurements should be taken and marked on the picture. Sometimes he allowed plans of buildings, and occasionally even points of the construction, to be placed 'at pleasure'. He wanted methods that were capable of giving an acceptable result in practice and he preferred to depict real objects, particularly buildings, rather than the abstract points, lines and figures discussed in many treatises. He insisted that as far as artists were concerned, perspective was a practical subject. To enable his audience to study it for themselves, he often named his sources and occasionally gave a full reference.

The early versions of lecture 3 are extremely long and it seems that the lecture was eventually split into two, with the latter part presented in the subsequent lecture (and the material in the early drafts of lecture 4 abandoned). It is not certain exactly where the split was made, so the material presented below could have been part of either lecture in the 1811 course.[66]

Turner continued with a selection of techniques for 'curvilinear' objects, particularly circles and capitals. He attributed these to a variety of sources, including Malton, Androuet du Cerceau, Sirigatti and Moxon. Most of his accounts are perfectly acceptable and, in the main, faithfully, if briefly, represent the approaches of the treatises from which they were taken. The exception is Sirigatti's method for depict-

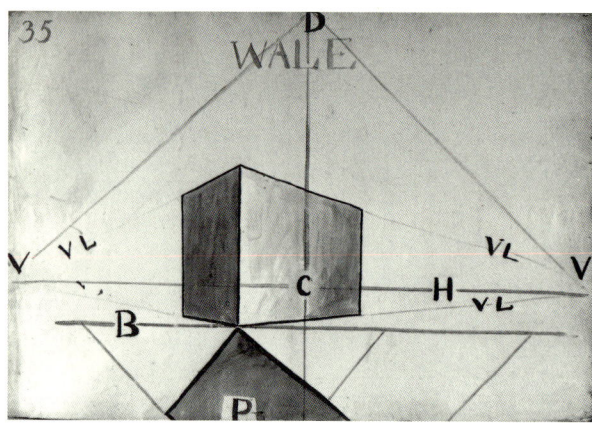

fig.39 'Basic Perspective Method for a Rectangular Object', lecture diagram 35 c.1810

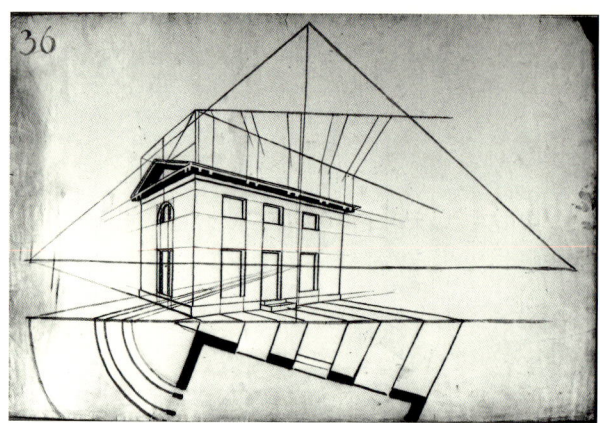

fig.40 'Basic Perspective Construction of a House', lecture diagram 36 (see also fig.41) c.1810

fig.41 'A House in Perspective', lecture diagram 36 (see also fig.40) c.1810

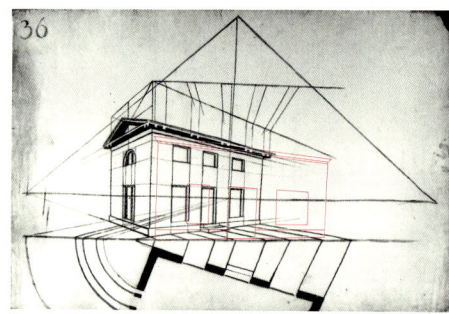

fig.42 Turner's perspective construction of a house (fig.40), with correct standard perspective representation overlaid (modern diagram)

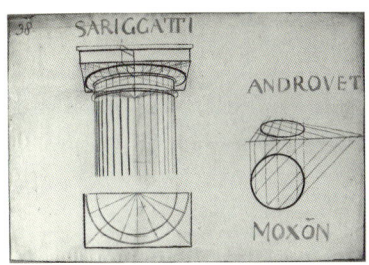

fig.43 'Sirigatti's Method for a Tuscan Capital, and a Method for a Circle Attributed to Moxon and Androuet du Cerceau', lecture diagram 38 (partly from Lorenzo Sirigatti, *La pratica della prospettiva*, 1596, pl.32) c.1810

ing a Tuscan capital (fig.43), which Turner completely misunderstood. He became so frustrated in his attempts to describe this method that he made an increasingly hostile series of criticisms. On first encountering it, he commented: 'The endless and overbearing confusion of points here must be a disadvantage.'[67] Later, he attacked it in humorous tone, punning on Sirigatti's examples of staircases and fiddles:[68] 'The multifarious lines may well be sufficient to many without enquiring whether they are all necessary or not in … parallel [perspective] and justly conclude they must be quite puzzled in angular staircases, and quickly determine not to climb Sirigatti's stairs … or play upon his fiddle.'[69] By the time the 1811 lecture was ready he had decided that Sirigatti's complexity was no joking matter. He abandoned his earlier wit and added a strict rejoinder: 'My position [is] that the complicated appearances which simple forms are often made to assume tend more to ingeniously perplex than to clear the way to a study, which when thoroughly known appears so simple as even to impeach common intellects for having once considered it complicated.'[70] These comments show that Turner found it difficult to understand complex methods of perspective, but also reflect a genuine desire to keep the subject simple. He explained that in his own diagrams he had omitted many details in order to keep them clear and to the point.

Next, Turner presented a long series of recommendations about the best procedures to adopt when depicting the architectural orders, illustrated by many diagrams. In the early drafts he first discussed how to depict various parts of the Tuscan order (figs.44–5 on p.49): the entablature, the shaft, various parts of the capital, and the pedestal. He then explained the Ionic, followed by the Corinthian capital (figs.46–7) and entablature. Throughout, he displayed a wide knowledge of specialist architectural terminology and approached his material confidently, writing with an authoritative tone. As usual, he did not set out every stage of each method, but outlined the best approaches to take in each case.

'Having passed through the orders … we will proceed to apply them as parts … in a regular building.'[71] For this, Turner chose the example of Robert Adam's Pulteney Bridge in Bath (figs.48–9), 'a building not selected for the beauty of its architecture, but from its possessing the principles of the square and circle, and having columns and entablature in projecting colonnades'.[72] To depict it he adopted a method known as a 'measure-point' type, rather than the plan-based type he had earlier used to depict a house. Throughout the lectures Turner consistently attributed measure-point methods to Thomas Malton Junior, but they are fairly common in perspective treatises. Although the method is complex, Turner succeeded in explaining it perfectly adequately.

Because of the way in which lectures 3 and 4 were rearranged, it is not clear how either of them ended in the 1811 course. In their earlier versions, they both finish with comments about the overall value of standard perspective. The early versions of lecture 3 finish with a fairly subtle critique of the way standard perspective represents high buildings.[73] As part of this critique, Turner developed the qualifications made in lecture 2 about the extent to which rules should be followed. For example: 'Supposing that the lines of each object are in the first instance produced by the rules heretofore laid down, yet deviations must be considered admissable',[74] to give an effect closer to the appearance of nature.

Turner completed his presentation of perspective in the early versions of lecture 4 by explaining that the artist's duty was to use perspective wisely. When 'the appearance of nature and the rules of art do vary, it is here the true artist must poise all the mechanical excellence of rules and the contrarities which are to [be] found in nature, with them to balance well the line between deformity and truth; and, in the words of our late, worthy keeper Wilton, it is betwixt the little more and the little less we must expect only to find propriety.'[75]

fig.46 'Corinthian Capital in Perspective', lecture diagram 53 c.1810

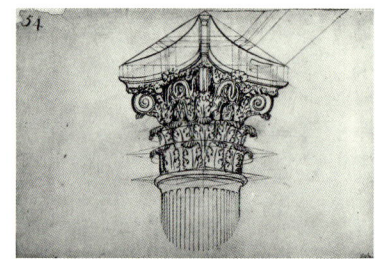

fig.47 'Perspective Construction of a Corinthian Capital', lecture diagram 54 c.1810

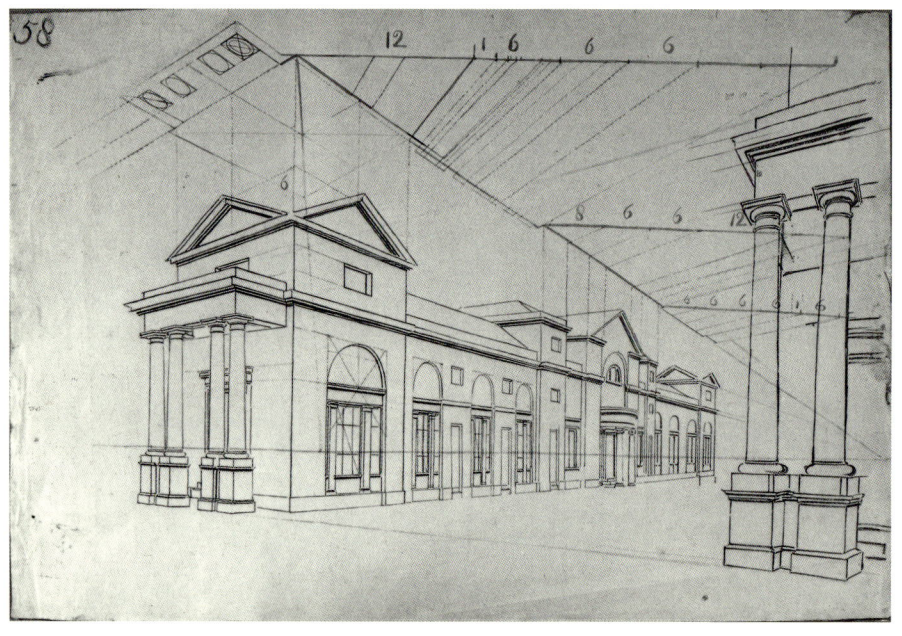

fig.48 'Perspective Construction of Pulteney Bridge, Bath', lecture diagram 58 c.1810

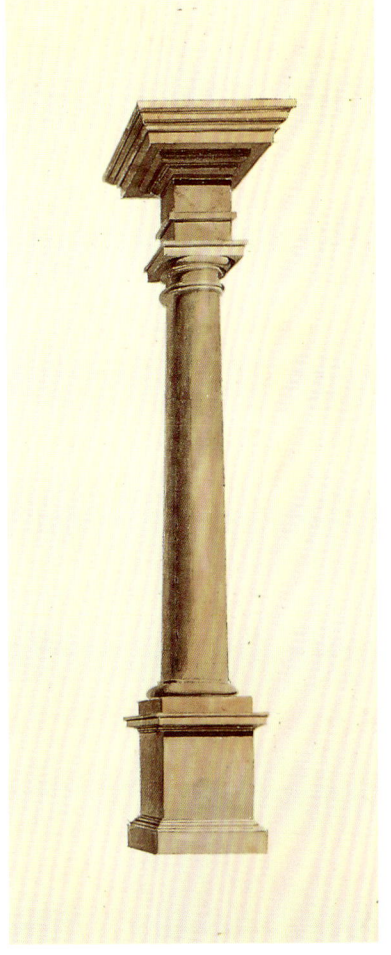

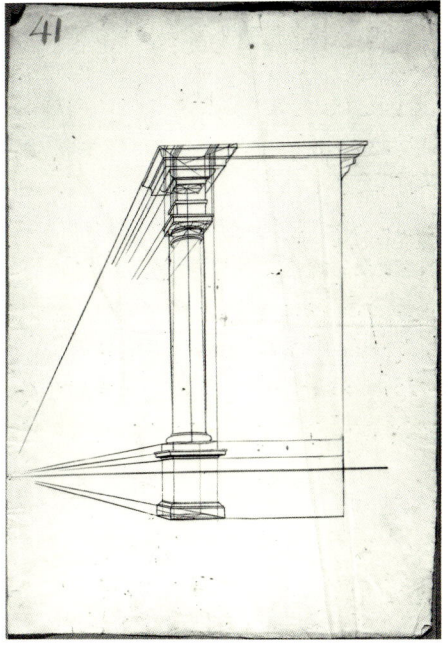

fig.44 'Tuscan Column in Perspective', lecture diagram 40 (detail) *c*.1810

fig.45 'Perspective Construction of a Tuscan Column', lecture diagram 41 *c*.1810

fig.49 'Pulteney Bridge, Bath, in Perspective', lecture diagram 59 *c*.1810

Lecture 5: Rules for Reflection and Refraction

'Like Picking Grains of Sand to Measure Time'

Turner's fifth lecture of 1811 was about 'reflexes' – or reflections – and their relationship to light and shade.[76] He reported that little had previously been written on the subject: 'It is possible that nothing is so difficult and undefined as the theory of reflexes, and yet they are [so] absolutely necessary to the painter's pursuit, that the neglect, even of an attempt, to establish some theory in most of the works of perspective is perhaps incomprehensible.' From one point of view, the neglect is 'probably most prudent, for to create doubts of what has hitherto been accepted is doing not only an injury to those who have written, but adding thorns in the way of the young student.'[77] However, Turner intended to display no such prudence: 'But to lament only and not endeavour to do something, when something is absolutely requisite, is perhaps of the two the worst; for even those doubts once explained may rouse a more minute investigation which may, in the end, discover positive axioms for reflexes … And he that attains it will deserve not only the thanks of those who follow him, but will obtain for himself a name that must be honoured as long as the English School exists … Each should boldly step towards adding to the branch [of study], and though he cannot flatter himself to attain the end, he must not be deterred from the attempt.'[78]

After this introduction, it is not surprising that what follows has an experimental flavour: much of the lecture seems to be a report of Turner's own direct observations and optical research.[79] A series of sketches in the first draft complements Turner's accounts of reflection, and probably formed the basis of large lecture diagrams. However, only a small number of such diagrams exist today.

After a brief summary of the theory of reflection, choosing a controversial version in which light is reflected in a small curve 'called the sphere of its activity',[80] Turner moved on to his central theme: that all surfaces, however dull, reflect some light. As a result, all objects are simultaneously lit from many directions, and with many qualities of light. Therefore, analyses based on a single light source are inappropriately simplistic. For example, shadows are never 'total shade' as long as 'any angle of light reflected and refracted can reach an opposite plane'.[81] A series of sketches (fig.50) forms part of his exploration of the ways in which light is reflected between various permutations of flat surfaces arranged opposite and adjacent to each other. One of the difficulties of talking about light and shade is that language cannot capture its complexity and subtlety: 'It is surely not possible to use

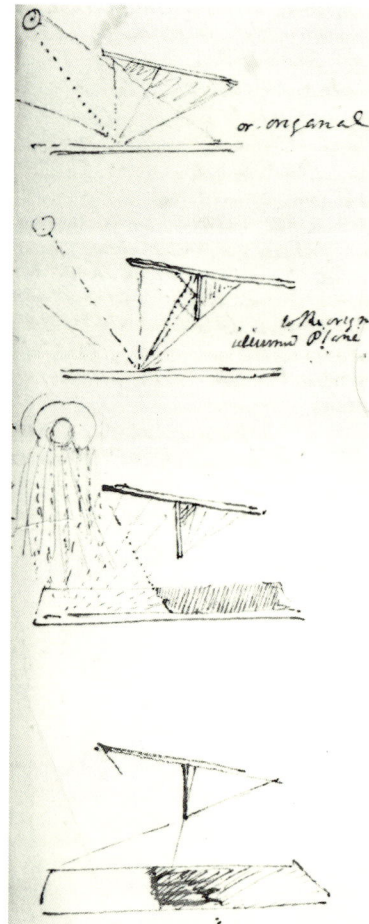

fig.50 Manuscript of first draft of lecture 5, studies of light reflected between adjacent plane surfaces *c*.1809

terms for reflexes sufficiently succinct for all the various lights and qualities of shade without intruding upon the term "darkness" when total privation of light is not meant, or calling a plane "in shade" where shadows are not formed.'[82]

Having qualified the terminology he was forced to use, Turner compared three kinds of reflections: '[ones from] solid bodies whose surfaces are uniformly opaque; those of polished bodies; [and those] of transparent bodies by glass or water.' In the case of an opaque surface, 'any part ... opposed to the sun receives and transmits in every angle, while the polished ones concentrate the ray on the part most immediately in opposition to it, and reflect it only in a point.'[83] A further variable is the position from which a surface is viewed. Consider a window: 'Windows illumined by the sun at any period of the day cast reflected light in all directions, according to [their] irregular-waved surface ... We frequently see the disc [of the sun] on each pane of glass that presents its proper angle, but at a distance the same window would appear in a glare of light – even at that extreme distance where form is lost.'[84] In the first draft, Turner added the couplet: 'Where form is lost in rising evening haze/ Full to the sun the village windows blaze.'[85]

The difference between dull surfaces and polished ones could be seen by comparing differently polished suits of armour. Turner gave examples from paintings, including Van Dyck's '1st Earl of Stafford' at Petworth, the 'bright lights and reflexes' of which he contrasted with Rembrandt's depiction of 'an old cuirass' which, with its 'semi-tones of indented and partly rusted iron' is divested 'of that high-light, double reflexes and deep shadow of the Stafford portrait'.[86] Rembrandt, 'whose discernment always equalled his judgement', succeeded in representing 'that second medium of dry light, so peculiarly the character of half-polished surfaces. For in nature, the higher bodies are polished, the more they reflect light and receive reflexes: their middle tones are less, but darker. While [for] those of decayed polish the first light is less brilliant, but more extended; the middle tones are broader, possessing light and colour ... receiving no reflexes but common light and shadow.'[87] Next came a brief consideration of the reflecting qualities of different metals in which tin, brass, copper, silver and gold were all mentioned.

Turner had some new proposals about the way reflections from water should be examined: 'Water has hitherto been said to be the same as polished bodies. Generally it may be considered as such, but abstractly [it is] quite different: first, from colour; secondly, from motion; and thirdly, its reflections, which admit of such endless variety, incomprehensible contrarieties and exhibit such phenomena, that it imperiously demands more attention than the dismissal it has generally received: "Water, like other transparent bodies may be treated the same, it being like a mirror." True, it is a mirror, but of nature's choicest work. Do we ever trace the double tones and prismatic reflected ray of the glass, or do we see the liquid melting reflection, or the gentle breeze that on the surface of the waters sleeps?'[88] He used a watercolour of the 'Fall of the Clyde' to illustrate part of his discussion of water's reflecting properties.[89] In general, he believed that all reflected light possesses colour, even that from dull surfaces, which is 'tinged but slightly with their colour'.[90] However, he said that he did not wish to go much further into the subject here, in part because of its complexity. So, 'having stated my idea as to the nature and diversity of reflexes, the more immediate effects of each must therefore be the object of our present enquiries.'[91] These 'more immediate effects' were the differences between, 'lights on plane surfaces ... in the open air' and those 'of daylight which are in confined places [and] assume the quality of positive shadows'.[92] Turner again observed how objects are illuminated by multiple light sources, resulting from reflection (and refraction) from every surface and even 'clouds, air etc'. Indoor shadows can be 'dissipated',[93] and are affected by alterations in the position of objects and the way light enters the room. As a final flourish he described the appearance of reflections produced *indoors* by water! The accompanying diagrams in the first draft seem to be analyses of the results of Turner's own observations.

His next subject, reflections and refractions in globes, seems equally experimental. Opaque, unpolished spheres 'receive reflected light in every situation either from daylight, from a reflecting surface, or from

fig.51 'Reflections in a Single Polished Metal Globe and in a Pair of Polished Metal Globes', lecture diagram *c*.1810

fig.52 'Reflections in a Transparent Globe', lecture diagram c.1810

their forms.'[94] He explored reflected light in: a polished metallic sphere (fig.51, left-hand side), in which 'the highest light ... partakes of the forms of the apertures' through which light entered the room; 'transparent circular bodies' (fig.52), drawing attention to the depiction of the effect in a Van Dyck portrait;[95] and a globe half-filled with water. He went into considerable detail, but felt his work to be quite inadequate: 'These attempts to define the powers of light and shade upon such changing surfaces as transparent bodies [are] like picking grains of sand to measure time, when these bodies are supposed to be surrounded with others.'[96] In his subsequent investigation of reflections in and between a pair of spheres he seemed confident enough about two solid spheres (fig.51, right-hand side) and simple transparent spheres. But when he reached 'clear transparent bodies part-filled with water', in spite of producing a diagram (fig.53), he felt that rules had been taken beyond their limits: 'Although we may feel to want further assistance and the help of rules, but it is here where the mind must work for its own reward and where given rules beyond general theoretical inductions would be useless, and the point where it becomes useless to prescribe methods to those who have no talents; and those who have talents will find methods for themselves, says Sir Joshua, dictated to them by their own particular attention and by their own ... particular opinions, derived from their observations and necessities.'[97]

Here the early drafts of the lecture end, but it seems to have been augmented with further material for the 1811 course. A review records that 'in the progress of the lecture he made some judicious remarks in the nature of genius and taste, and relieved the unavoidable dryness of an abstract discourse by occasional citations of poetry.'[98]

fig.53 'Reflections and Refractions in Two Transparent Globes, One Half-filled with Water', lecture diagram c.1810

Lecture 6: Landscape Painting Reviewed

'Backgrounds: Introduction of Architecture and Landscape'

According to a contemporary, Turner's final lecture of 1811 was 'more general' than the other five.[99] In his original plan, Turner had proposed to examine 'Backgrounds: Introduction of architecture and landscape',[100] a subject not unknown to eighteenth- and early nineteenth-century perspective treatises, but in the event he cast his net rather wider. His concluding subject for 1811 was landscape painting in general: he pronounced on its role and surveyed the work of many earlier artists. The lecture, now generally known as the 'Backgrounds' lecture, has been published in full, so there is no need to set it out in detail here.[101]

However, it is worth noting that the lecture does not completely ignore linear perspective. For example, towards the beginning Turner repeated the comments he had made in his first lecture about the fundamental importance of perspective in the design of Raphael's cartoons: 'In the "Paul Preaching at Athens" [fig.54] ... perspective introductions were essential to the subject, and by means of the high[102] horizon and the steps, only Paul possesses that elevation which, together with the simple yet energetic form, commands that attention by situation, and which the nature of the subject demanded. And if we

fig.54 Raphael, 'Cartoon for the Tapestry of St Paul Preaching at Athens' *c.*1515–16

fig.55 'Geometry of the Figure of St Paul in Raphael's "St Paul Preaching at Athens"', lecture diagram *c.*1812–28

fig.56 Martino Rota after Titian, 'The Martyrdom of St Peter' [n.d.]

were to divest the lines of light, shade and colour, Paul would hold the same power of elevation by lines only.'[103] In a later version of the lecture (although probably not in 1811[104]) Turner may have shown a diagram that demonstrates the further linear framework on which Paul himself is based (fig.55). He pointed out a few other aspects of perspective in pictures, praising the 'deep-sunk horizon' of Titian's 'St Peter Martyr' (fig.56) and Poussin's use of parallel perspective, which demonstrates 'the necessity of such rules to produce propriety, even in landscape'.[105] However, these references are few and far between. Furthermore, most of them are in additions to the lecture texts, not the first draft. The lecture originally contained next to nothing about the subject with which Turner was supposed to concern himself as professor of perspective.[106]

Turner ended lecture 6, and thus his 1811 course as a whole, by reminding his students of the responsibilities that they faced:

'To you, therefore, young gentlemen, must the nation look for the further advancement of the profession. All that have toiled up the steep ascent have left in their advancement footsteps of value to succeeding assailants. You will mark them as positions or beacons in your course. To you, therefore, this institution offers its instructions and consigns their efforts, looking forward with the hope that ultimately the joint endeavours of concording abilities will, in the pursuit of all that is meritorious, irrevocably fix the united standard of the arts in the British Empire.'[107]

CHAPTER 3   PAINTER OF PERSPECTIVE

Ignorance or Indifference? Turner's Practical Perspective Skills

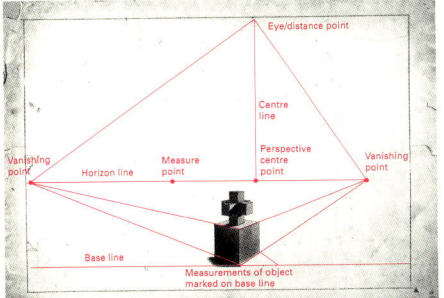

fig.57 'Perspective Study of a Cross on a Cube', preparatory study for a lecture diagram c.1810 (with elements of construction emphasised)

fig.61 'Radley Hall' 1789 (with elements of construction emphasised)

'St George's, Bloomsbury', lecture diagram 7 c.1810 (detail of fig.92)

Conflicting verdicts have been reached about Turner's practical abilities in perspective. In 1902, Sir Walter Armstrong declared: 'A very short examination of any picture or drawing of his in which architecture is an important feature is enough to show that his real knowledge of perspective was confined to a few of its more easily mastered principles.' Armstrong did allow that 'it is possible that he may have had clearer ideas than those he managed to convey, whether in words or with his pencil, and that his practical mistakes sprang rather from indifference than from ignorance.'[1] On the other hand, in 1905, W.L. Wyllie, himself an artist who studied perspective, wrote: 'There can be no doubt that Turner thoroughly understood the principles and practice of the science.' In fact, Turner could not have painted many of his pictures 'unless he had perspective at his fingers' ends'.[2] These two statements seem incompatible; is either of them true?

It is clear from Turner's perspective lectures that he was familiar with an extremely wide variety of perspective methods. He was also able to apply some of these techniques in practice, as demonstrated by some studies he made while preparing his large lecture illustrations. In these studies Turner painstakingly produced geometrically rigorous perspective representations of simple three-dimensional shapes, architectural details and even entire buildings. He carried out a large amount of constructional drawing: measurements are marked off with compasses, angles are measured, ruled lines predominate – it seems that nothing was left to be determined by eye.[3]

For one preliminary perspective study, Turner used a full 'measure-point' method (similar to the procedure he demonstrated in his lecture diagram of Pulteney Bridge, fig.48) to depict a three-dimensional cross standing on a cube. To indicate the complexity of the procedure that Turner had to employ to represent even this simple object in perspective, part of the geometrical construction that the drawing contains is emphasised in figure 57. There is a horizon line, a base line and a centre line, with the eye/distance point located where the centre line meets the ruled frame of the drawing. Two lines drawn from this eye/distance point give the two vanishing points on the horizon, each near to the left or right edge of the drawing. The measure point corresponding to the right-hand vanishing point is clearly marked, also on the horizon.[4] Various measurements of the object are set off on the base line and, as expected, lines can be found from these to the measure point and the vanishing points. There are several other parts of the construction that can be identified, but those outlined here are enough to demonstrate that a comprehensive perspective technique has been used.

fig.58 'Perspective Study of a Doric Entablature', preparatory study for lecture diagrams c.1810

Turner was also able to depict accurately more complex objects, such as a Doric entablature (fig.58). For this impressive work he selected a perspective centre point near to the bottom right-hand corner of the sheet and set off accurate measurements of the entablature on a horizontal line across the top of the drawing. He used these to produce, near the top of the sheet, a plan of the object in perspective. This plan was built up with great care and includes details such as the exact position of each part of each triglyph. He constructed the final representation of the entablature directly beneath the plan and then added the shadows.[5]

Some of the finished lecture illustrations were based directly on careful drawings such as these; for example, one of the illustrations of a house for his third lecture (fig.41) is a coloured tracing from a painstaking perspective construction. Occasionally the original proved too small: there is a meticulous pencil drawing of Pulteney Bridge, and a tracing from it (figs.59, 60), but the final diagrams are much larger (figs. 48–9).[6] Figure 48 includes details of a perspective construction, but it is simplified from the one Turner carried out initially. In other lecture diagrams, the method shown is completely different from that used for the preparatory study.[7]

fig.59 'Perspective Study of Pulteney Bridge, Bath', preparatory study for lecture diagrams c.1810

The careful preparatory drawings demonstrate that Turner did not loose the skills he had acquired when he trained as an architectural draughtsman, long before he became professor of perspective. In addition to his time with Thomas Malton Junior, he worked for the architect Thomas Hardwick, for whom he produced architectural drawings.[8] However, in spite of Turner's skills, surviving drawings from this period show no evidence of the use of full perspective constructions. Rather, Turner often based his finished works on freehand sketches, which he squared for transfer. For example, as part of a job for Hardwick Turner squared-up a pencil drawing of Wanstead New Church (TB IV A). In this some lines are ruled, but others are not; and the ruled lines themselves seem to be on top of less precise ones. Unfortunately the finished drawing based on this study is lost and it is not known whether Turner carried out a full perspective construction for it. But this seems unlikely: in some of Turner's early finished architectural works, such as a view of Radley Hall (fig.61 on p.57), vanishing

fig.60 'Pulteney Bridge, Bath, in Perspective', tracing from fig.59 c.1810

fig.62 'The Pantheon, Oxford Street, the Morning after the Fire' RA 1792

points were used, but they seem to have been located by eye and there is no evidence of the application of an accurate perspective construction.⁹ Several years later, Turner squared for transfer an extremely rough pencil sketch of the Pantheon, Oxford Street (TB CXCV 156), which formed the basis of a finished watercolour exhibited at the Royal Academy in 1792 (fig.62). It is, of course, possible that now-lost accurate perspective constructions intervened between Turner's quick sketches and his finished watercolours, but there is no evidence of this. His use of a ruler and vanishing points in finished works of the late 1780s and early 1790s was merely to tidy up the information he had collected freehand in his sketches and not to produce rigorously accurate perspective views.

Later in the 1790s, when Turner depicted more elaborate buildings, particularly interiors, he often prepared a ruled framework, over which he added details. These frameworks sometimes make use of a few measurements, sometimes even a vanishing point, but they do not amount to anything like a full perspective construction of the type he was to demonstrate in his lectures. For his drawing of the interior of the hall of Christ Church, Oxford (fig.63) Turner determined the angles of many elements of the building with the aid of a carefully drawn network of ruled pencil lines that converge to the perspective centre point (near the left-hand side), which serves (perfectly correctly) as the vanishing point for those lines perpendicular to the picture plane. With very few exceptions, all elements of the building that should converge

fig.63 'The Interior of the Hall of Christ Church, Oxford' c.1798–1804

to this point do so, and Turner made corrections to ensure that this is so.[10] Other lines are also carefully drawn: the back wall of the hall includes ruled lines, and others assist in the positioning of the tops of the windows in the bay. Also, some measurements seem to have been marked off: for example, to space the window mullions and the coats of arms on the end wall. However, there is no sign that Turner used measurements of the building itself in preparing the drawing, and it should not be thought that the presence of a vanishing point and a ruled framework signifies that a full technique of perspective has been used. Far from it, the ruled lines simply served to make a depiction based on observation (rather than construction) neater and more controlled. Furthermore, when Turner produced a finished watercolour from this drawing, in preparation for an engraving, he altered the proportions of the room, widening it and lowering the roof. This would have made a nonsense of any attempts at rigorous perspective accuracy in the initial drawing. Indeed, Turner's lack of fidelity to his motif was noted by the committee that commissioned the watercolour, who criticised its 'topographical inaccuracy'.[11]

In some apparently carefully constructed drawings the ruled framework does not even make accurate use of vanishing points and is therefore inconsistent with even the most rudimentary application of a rigorous perspective method. In another Oxford drawing, this time of the interior of New College Chapel (fig.64), although there is an exten-

fig.65 'Cassiobury' c.1807

fig.66 'Ely Cathedral – The Interior of the Octagon' 1794

fig.64 'The Interior of New College Chapel, Oxford' c.1798–1801

sive network of ruled lines, the lines perpendicular to the picture plane do not recede to a consistent point.[12] Similarly, although Turner used a ruler to depict many parts of his view of the exterior of Cassiobury, a house remodelled by James Wyatt in 1800 (fig.65), the lines of the building do not meet at vanishing points. And, even with their limited degree of precision, these works are exceptional: usually Turner did not employ ruled lines at all. He drew completely freehand, and with great skill. It is hard to believe that a drawing as large and detailed as 'The Octagon at Ely' (fig.66) was drawn without some kind of mechanical assistance, but it contains not a single ruled line and certainly bears no sign of any perspective construction. Nor is it possible that a drawing aid like a camera obscura was used, as the scene depicted is not one that can be taken from a single viewpoint. Thus, it seems to have been drawn freehand, on the spot.[13] (Although this does raise the question of why Turner made use of a ruled framework to guide him in works such as the Oxford interiors, but not in this one.)

'The Octagon at Ely' does not represent a view that can be seen from a single viewpoint, and 'Interior of the Hall of Christ Church, Oxford' is topographically inaccurate. These facts highlight a key characteristic of Turner's approach to depicting the world: he had no desire to show an exact, 'photographic' view of a building or scene. Turner's finished works are often based on material contained in several sketches, each taken from a different position. Even individual sketches can incorporate views taken from several places, or deliberately alter the lie of the land or details of architecture. Turner rarely sketched a landscape without altering its topography.[14] But this does not mean that he ignored the motif before him. Ruskin argued that every line in one of Turner's sketches 'indicates something that is really there, only everything is shifted and sorted into the exact places that Turner chose'.[15] Elsewhere Ruskin noted what Turner achieved by doing this: 'All mathematical, and arithmetical, and generally scientific truth, is ... truth of the husk and surface, hard and shallow; and only the imaginative truth is precious ... those who want to know the real facts of the world's outside aspect, will find that they cannot trust maps, nor charts, nor any manner of mensuration; the most important facts being quite immeasurable, and that ... the Turnerian topography is the only one to be trusted.'[16] While the direct observation of the visual world provided the basis of Turner's art, he went beyond appearances to abstract the essence, the ideal, the central forms of nature.[17] This idealism was crucial in determining his attitude to standard perspective, the *raison d'être* of which is to represent scenes and objects from a single fixed viewpoint with mathematical accuracy.

In his *Pre-Raphaelitism* of 1851, Ruskin noted: 'I have never met but with two men in my life who knew enough of perspective ... Our architects certainly do not, and it was but the other day that, talking to one of the most distinguished among them, the author of several most valuable works, I found he actually did not know how to draw a circle in perspective.'[18] So Turner's avoidance of rigorous geometrical perspective was not particularly unusual (although some of the ways in which he manipulated it were). It certainly did not prevent him from depicting space extremely successfully, and he was tremendously skilled at depicting the form and volume of buildings. Indeed, his skills were highly regarded by architects, and he was commissioned to prepare architectural perspective drawings. For example, in 1798 a perspective view of Fonthill Abbey by Turner was exhibited at the Royal Academy under the name of its architect, James Wyatt.[19] By the mid-1790s Turner was able to create views of buildings, particularly the interiors of cathedrals, breathtaking in their representation of not only architectural solidity, but also space and light (figs.66, 95).

The Foundation of Art: Perspective in the Design of Turner's Pictures

As professor of perspective Turner had a duty to provide a thorough account of perspective, and he gave a much greater role to methods and rules in his lectures than he did in his practice. He argued: 'Without the aid of perspective, art totters at its very foundation.'[20] But the belief in perspective he expressed in the lectures is not simply platitude or hypocrisy,[21] for perspective does play a crucial role in Turner's art. While it would be inappropriate to analyse his use of it in terms of its geometrical accuracy, or the exact size and position of objects (as has been done so successfully for some other artists[22]), he almost always produced a completely coherent three-dimensional picture space (and usually one consistent with a view from a single point).

In his lectures Turner noted that perspective not only serves to depict and position individual objects, but also contributes to a picture's overall design. There is a 'distinction between the geometric laws of perspective regulating the parts, and the rules of perspective influencing the design.' In this latter category, the laws of perspective 'com-

left
fig.67 'Mainz' ?1840
right
fig.68 'Promenade with Figures' after 1837

pose each design into her arrangement'.²³ A critic records that Turner compared the work of Raphael and Dürer: they were 'each equally correct' in their use of perspective, but Turner 'advised a due concealment' of it. Indeed, Dürer, 'ostentatious of his acquirements, reduced most of his works to mere diagrams', while Raphael 'most judiciously conceals the laboured lines of his perspective ... although the rules may all be traced, yet their effects are not made prominent.'²⁴

In Turner's own pictures perspective plays a role similar to the latter: it does not dominate them, but provides their 'foundations'. In a study of Mainz (fig.67), pencil lines establish the picture space. They clearly determine the recession of the bridge that dominates the left-hand side and also confirm the angle of the far bank of the river to the right of the centre. Further pencil drawing locates part of the nearmost bank of the river at the extreme right-hand edge of the picture. In this study there is, of course, no attempt at 'accurate' perspective, but controlled recession underlies the whole work. Many of Turner's pencil or pen-and-ink compositional studies demonstrate the importance of linear perspective in structuring space,²⁵ as do many of his slightest studies, such as a colour structure of figures walking on a promenade (fig.68). The dominant visual pull of the receding promenade is reinforced by the direction of the brushstrokes, and the picture space is further defined by some delicate pencilwork suggesting buildings in perspective in the background.

These pictures (figs.67–8) are but two examples among many of Turner's adoption of a central perspective scheme, in which the main compositional element, such as a promenade, road or bridge, is perpendicular to the picture plane. Lines perpendicular to the picture plane converge to a point known as the 'perspective centre point', which is always directly opposite the artist's eye.²⁶ In the simplest form of central composition, the perspective centre point is chosen to coincide with the physical centre of the picture and the artist is situated at the centre of the road, etc. In this case, the road will be in the middle of the picture, dividing it symmetrically in two (figs.69–71).²⁷ If the artist is not in the centre of the road then it will not recede symmetrically – the side of it further away from the artist will converge more steeply than the other.

The perspective centre can be placed to one side of the picture, implying the artist was not at the centre of the picture when it was produced (figs.67–8, 72–4). Dürer often did this, a fact which Turner noted: 'If we look back to the prints of Albert Dürer we shall find that he moved the central point ... from the centre of his picture to give diversity of line.'²⁸ This was discussed by Edward Edwards, Turner's predecessor at the Royal Academy, who recommended positioning viewpoints near to the centre, and praised Poussin for doing this. Com-

fig.69 'Entrance to the Little Chartreuse' 1802

fig.70 'Pass of Splügen' c.1841

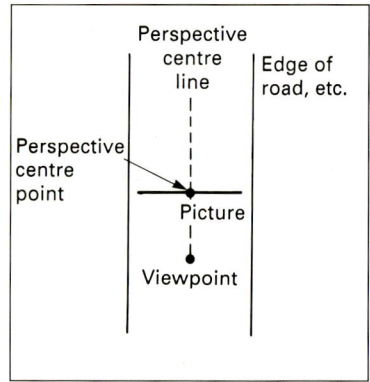
fig.71 Perspective structure of figs.69–70 (modern diagram)

fig.72 'The Road from Voreppe to Grenoble' 1802

PAINTER OF PERSPECTIVE

fig.73 'Palazzo Tasca-Papafava, Venice' ?1840

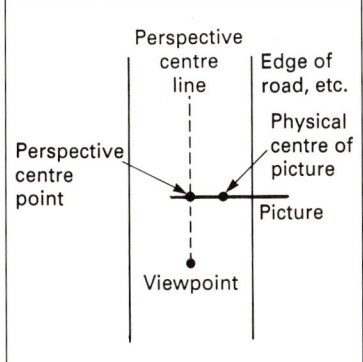

fig.74 Perspective structure of figs.72–3 (modern diagram)

fig.75 'Bellinzona from the Road to Locarno' c.1841

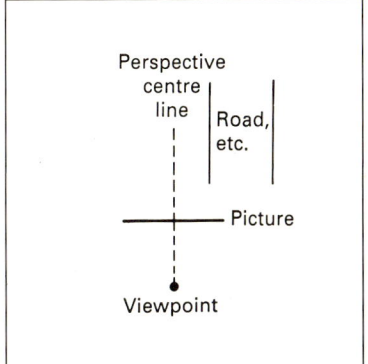

fig.76 Perspective structure of fig.75 (modern diagram)

paring painting to the theatre, Edwards observed: 'No man will prefer a side view if he can procure a centre seat.'[29] However, Turner did not depend solely on central viewpoints: in many of his pictures the perspective centre point is close to the left or right edge.

In principle, the centre could be completely outside the bounds of the picture, but even Turner was critical of this, decrying it as 'reprehensible' and an 'aberration',[30] and he did not do it himself. Yet another effect is obtained if the artist is positioned completely outside the road so that, although the road is perpendicular to the picture, it heads towards or away from the picture's physical centre, sometimes quite dramatically (figs.75–6).

Sometimes Turner used central perspective to focus the composition in a single direction (figs.69, 75), but on other occasions he provided other 'routes' for the eye to follow (fig.67), or at least allowed it to move gently in directions other than that established by the central recession (fig.72). Many of Turner's exhibited oils include a firm central recession, but still allow the viewer to explore other areas of the picture without impediment. In 'Calais Pier' (fig.77) equal visual weight is given to the perpendicular pier at the right and to the swelling sea at the left. The way in which the pier recedes situates the viewer on it, and draws us towards the disembarking passengers; but our position is not secure – the sea attracts the eye just as forcefully, and threatens to suck us into the water, away from the solid rectilinearity of the wooden pier.

'Frosty Morning' (fig.78) is less dramatic, but structured in a similar way: the road firmly leads the eye to the distant stage-coach, but the option remains of following the softer direction, established by the angle of the horse and cart and wheelbarrow, to pass over the low fence and enter the field beyond. In 'Palestrina – Composition' (fig.79) there are three different routes that the eye can follow: down the avenue at the right, over the bridge to the town at the left, or along the central river. Unusually for Turner, the viewer's position in this picture is not explicit. The road, river and bridge all seem to be equally close as the picture is viewed, so it is not clear where to stand. A further difficulty in exploring the picture space is the 'unseen cascade' that the eye must cross before it can reach the distant view.[31]

Much has been written about the effect of these multiple vistas, drawing attention to contrasting natural and manmade routes, whether they are open to the horizon or blocked, and the differing speeds with which they draw the eye.[32] They have been presented here as examples of the ways in which a subtle deployment of perspective underpins Turner's compositions. His deep understanding of perspective enabled him to produce extremely complex picture spaces that were completely consistent in their recession. Every inch of depth is clearly

[65]

fig.77 'Calais Pier, with French Poissards Preparing for Sea: An English Packet Arriving' exh.1803

fig.78 'Frosty Morning' exh.1813

fig.79 'Palestrina – Composition' 1828

fig.80 'Harfleur' c.1832

fig.81 'Bridge at Meulan' c.1832

fig.82 'Isis' 1819

demarcated and the spectator can explore the entire picture without experiencing any alarming discontinuities (fig.80).

There are further ways in which Turner exploited perspective effects. He occasionally reinforced recession through the arrangement of figures or animals, such as the firmly aligned dogs in 'Petworth Park: Tillington Church in the Distance' (fig.121), the curving but centralised flight of birds in 'Shade and Darkness – The Evening of the Deluge' (fig.132) and the figures pulling on a rope in 'Bridge at Meulan' (fig.81). But perspective is never allowed to dominate. Where recession threatens to drag a composition in a single direction, it is often counterbalanced with an object parallel to the picture plane, such as a Claudian bridge (fig.82), a frontally placed building (fig.67), or a piece of masonry, the vertical triangle of which counteracts the triangles into depth of perspective recession (fig.82). With devices such as these, Turner stabilised his compositions and concealed his perspective, preventing it from turning his pictures into 'mere diagrams'.

Perspective for Grandeur and Elevation

Balance and stability were essential to history painting, which still occupied the highest position in the academic hierarchy in the early nineteenth century. Turner's careful use of perspective to create coherent picture spaces played a part in his attempt to raise the status of modern landscape painting, in part by imbuing it with the features of history painting. According to seventeenth- and eighteenth-century theories of pictorial composition, a dominant centre concentrates interest and contributes to the unity of effect in a picture. Some theorists went further and required the most important elements and action to be located near the centre and a picture to be capable of being taken in at a single glance. The centrality of a picture can be enhanced by the perspective scheme and central perspective can play a much greater role than simply providing a pleasing route for the eye to follow: it can help order the picture, particularly if the physical and perspective centres coincide.

The rules about unity were not hard and fast, and some artists, particularly landscape painters, deliberately broke them (and Turner certainly did not adopt them in full).[33] Nevertheless, in the early nineteenth century, central compositions offered one approach to raising the standing of landscape painting. Turner employed many types of composition, and centralised ones represent only a part of his output. But they are an important part, and the simple device of having a road receding at ninety degrees to the picture plane is only one of the ways in which he produced them. He also drew on factors other than perspective, not least the sun. In some works the reflections it creates in water are tantamount to a road receding (fig.83); in others, shadows radiating from the sun further strengthen the picture space (figs. 84–5); sometimes the central sun and the shadows it creates dominate the entire image (fig.86).

Central perspective is part of what Turner called 'parallel perspective': the depiction of objects, particularly buildings, with their main faces parallel and perpendicular to the picture plane. Then, lines are either parallel to the picture surface (and so do not converge), or are perpendicular to it and converge to the perspective centre point – the sole vanishing point in parallel perspective. Indeed, Turner called the centre 'the principle of the parallel'.[34] Parallelism of form is an important element in neo-classical history painting and it was strongly recommended in early nineteenth-century perspective treatises, partly because of the rigorous grid it creates.[35] In his lectures Turner also had much to say about the potential of parallel perspective: 'It gives …

plainness, elevation, simplicity and lines; frequently grandeur. This is [in] fact the sphere of its activity. This is the generic value of P.P. [parallel perspective]. Its qualities become the parallelism of form … It [?leaves] the situation of an accessory and becomes a principle in composition, and is most productive of grandeur through simplicity of form.'[36] He praised Raphael and Poussin as the artists most successful in exploiting the effects of parallel perspective to obtain grandeur, and displayed particular admiration for Raphael's tapestry cartoons (fig.54): 'Never eccentric with littleness or affected by contrast, but always covered with unspeakable majesty by simplicity of lines and forms … simple grandeur and simplicity of composition … arrangement so truly appropriate and yet so appropriately easy.'[37] 'Contrast' – of which too much is apparently a bad thing – is created by 'angular perspective',

fig.83 'Stangate Creek on the River Medway' c.1824

fig.84 'Lausanne: Cathedral and Bridge' 1841

below left
fig.85 'View across the Campagna with a Low Sun' 1819
below
fig.86 'Figures in a Storm' ?after 1830

fig.87 'Regulus' 1828, reworked 1837

in which objects are set obliquely to the picture plane. While 'parallel all are made conducive of simplicity', 'angular ... produce contrast, or magnificence, or richness, or variety'.[38] Following the traditional divide, Turner compared Poussin and Rubens: 'Two masters, Poussin and Rubens, will be sufficient to show the different properties of lines in parallel and angular perspective. In the pictures of the former, a continual restraint to time, place, introductory, artificial and local arrangements appear; in the last scarcely any ... [in his] ingenious confusion of extraordinary powers.'[39] With their balanced compositions, Poussin and other exponents of parallel perspective come out best in the subsequent discussion of design, and throughout his lectures Turner stresses the benefits of arranging dominant objects parallel to the picture plane.

Turner's preference for parallel arrangements is evident in many of his historical oil paintings. From the works that deliberately echo Poussin such as 'The Tenth Plague of Egypt' (B&J 17), through seaports in which the sun further stresses the centre (figs.87, 108), to 'The Parting of Hero and Leander' (fig.97) and even 'Juliet and her Nurse' (B&J 365), and 'Rain, Steam and Speed' (B&J 409), parallel and perpendicular lines predominate. There are, of course, exceptions (particularly a group of paintings of the late 1830s[40]), but generally Turner strengthened the grandeur and unity of his historical works through his choice of 'the parallel principle'. In less architectural works, where the distinction between parallel and angular perspective is not strictly relevant, centrality, created by roads, etc., or by the sun, can perform a similar function.

Turner argued that the use of a low viewpoint could also produce grandeur, and care should be taken to position the horizontal line (which marks the height of the artist's eye) at an appropriate level: 'Since this line unquestionably produces character, it beholds the student well to consider what he wishes to be seen or hid, what quantity and quality his principal object should possess, and ... consider its intended effect.'[41] Referring to the copy of Raphael's 'Paul Preaching at Athens' (fig.54) hung before his audience in the Great Room of the Royal Academy, he observed: 'The dignity and commanding aspect of St Paul in the cartoon before you is proof of the quality of a low horizontal line to produce grandeur.' He continued: 'But if a stronger [proof] were necessary, "The Martyrdom of St Peter" by Titian would be convincing to everyone, even from the print [fig.56]. The horizontal line scarce rises a twentieth part from the base of the picture, the figure becomes colossal and [?heads] forwards, and the gigantic trees rush, as it were, into infinity.'[42]

This discussion is primarily concerned with history paintings that contain prominent figures and so has little bearing on Turner's own practice. He, in fact, made use of a wide range of viewing heights in his historical paintings, but some tendencies can be discerned in other categories of picture. For example, he regularly selected a low horizon for sea-pieces, where he often adopted the position of someone in a small boat, dwarfed by the swelling water. For topographical works, especially views of single buildings, he explained that it is the position of the horizontal line 'on which the aspect of the building depends, and on which the character, altitude, grandeur or extent ultimately relies.'[43] His use of a low viewpoint, often in combination with a parallel building (and a short viewing distance), is marked. In his earliest pictures, Turner tended to place buildings oblique to the picture plane, following the eighteenth-century conventions of artists such as the Maltons and Michael Angelo Rooker. Examples of this approach include Radley Hall (fig.61), and 'The Pantheon, Oxford Street, the Morning after the Fire' (fig.62). By 1796 and Llandaff Cathedral (fig.88) the viewpoint is significantly lower, although the building is still obliquely set. The figures are small to accentuate the height of the architecture. Soon afterwards Turner regularly positioned his picture parallel to the building he depicted. He did this for several of his views of Fonthill Abbey made in 1799 (fig.89), which clearly demonstrate Turner's growing tendency to dramatise the height of buildings through the choice of extremely low viewpoints and diminutive figures. A comparison between figure 89 and 'The Pantheon, Oxford Street' shows how Turner moved away from the topographical tradition during the 1790s in favour of towering frontality. In the later eighteenth century the use of angular perspective had been seen as a mark of skill by topographers.[44] But by 1800 Turner's skill was publicly established and he was able to focus his attention on increasing the grandeur of low-status topographical work. From 1800 onwards there are many parallel arrangements in Turner's works. Most of the architectural works in the *Liber Studiorum*, on which Turner worked from *c*.1807 onwards, are parallel to the picture plane; for example, 'Holy Island Cathedral' (fig.90) totally fills the picture with its frontality and low viewpoint. Turner regularly depicted Venetian buildings parallel to the picture (fig.91); usually depicted buildings in landscape so that they were parallel to the picture plane; and almost always placed his picture parallel to the walls when he depicted interiors of houses (although adopted more varied viewpoints for church interiors). As noted earlier, Turner often made use of bridges parallel to the picture plane – a device that not only serves to balance other aspects of a composition, but also directly reinforces its frontality.

fig.88 'Llandaff Cathedral: The West Front' 1795–6

fig.89 'Fonthill Abbey: South Front' 1799

fig.90 'Holy Island Cathedral' 1808

'Attaining Apparent Altitude'

To give an adequate sense of the height of buildings, Turner argued that artists should take account of the fact that 'vertical parallel lines diminish'.[45] Consider a tall building with vertical sides, such as the tower of a church. When viewing the tower from nearby, the sides do not appear parallel, but seem to converge together upwards – the tower appears narrower at the top than the bottom. This effect is now known as 'vertical convergence'. Turner explained: 'Whenever the eye is raised to an object, that object possess gradation and diminution at all angles [and] strictly not perpendicular [nor] parallel lines. It therefore recedes from the eye ... and I feel sometimes bold enough to assert, when I consult that stupendous fabric St Paul's Cathedral ... that only one horizontal and perpendicular line strictly speaking exist in nature.'[46] In this passage Turner observed that only the vertical line directly in front of the spectator appears perpendicular to the horizon – that is, truly vertical. (He also observed that only the horizon appears strictly horizontal – other horizontal lines are subject to what is now called 'lateral convergence', see below.)

In a standard perspective representation all the lines depicting the vertical sides of a building are parallel on the surface of the picture and so do not converge. In theory, this vertical convergence does not need to be shown on the picture surface of a standard perspective representation because the lines of the representation are themselves seen in perspective when the finished picture is viewed – the theoretical position is the same as that for marginal distortion.[47]

But Turner believed that the standard way of showing verticals as perpendicular to the bottom of the picture could never make objects appear high enough: 'Perpendicular lines from the base always give a squat, depressed appearance to all elevated objects.'[48] Again he considered the experience of viewing a London landmark: the towers of Westminster Abbey. Even at a distance of twice their height 'they appear to diminish, although we know their proportions are nearly equal at the top as at the base.'[49] As the viewer moves closer, 'they rapidly decrease upwards and approach towards horizontal perspective vertically, which is allowed an imaginary [vanishing] point.'[50] Turner recalled that Thomas Malton Junior told him that when he was preparing the plates for *A Picturesque Tour through the Cities of London and Westminster* (1792–1801) he was 'disappointed in the expectation of attaining the apparent altitude of the above-mentioned towers by putting them in lines in the usual way; namely, by making all verticals parallel.'[51] Turner noted with satisfaction that (unlike his father) Malton

fig.91 'The Ducal Palace: The Porta della Carta, Venice' ?1833

fig.92 'St George's, Bloomsbury', lecture diagram 7 c.1810

Junior 'had not the prejudice for rules so overbearing, so strong as to reject vision when in array against mechanical rules. [He] admitted against such rules.'[52] Turner recommended that artists should begin by following the rules of standard perspective, but feel at liberty to adapt the results if they proved unacceptable: 'Supposing that the lines of each object are in the first instance produced by the rules heretofore laid down, yet deviations must be considered admissible to assist the magnitude of supposed altitude.'[53] He noted that the majority of perspective treatises insisted that the rules should be strictly followed, and that, in order to avoid problems in standard perspective, many treatises recommended that viewpoints should not be too close – a restriction that Turner was not willing to accept. In spite of the exhortations of theorists, artists often did not represent verticals as strictly perpendicu-

fig.93 'The Grand Canal, Venice: The Rialto, the Palazzo Balbi on the Left' ?1840

lar to the bases of pictures. Thus, Turner was perhaps displaying more pragmatism than radicalism in his rejection of contemporary theoretical orthodoxies in his lectures.[54]

Turner 'admitted against' the standard rules in his own practice, but perhaps not as forcefully as his calls for disobedience may lead one to expect. There are a few instances of vertical convergence in the lecture diagrams. One, of St George's, Bloomsbury (fig.92) does not have strictly perpendicular sides to its tower. However, there appears to be no consistent system regulating the way in which they are shown. The side furthest from the picture plane (to the left in the picture) is straight and very nearly vertical. On the other hand, that part of the side at the right that is not hidden by the body of the church, slopes markedly to the left as it rises. The lines representing these two sides are largely straight, but the remaining one (central in the picture) twists rather uncomfortably. It begins its rise from the ground by leaning a little to the right, then changes direction and heads to the left, next giving a definite bulge to the tower before it heads upwards, again to the right. The treatment of the columns of the pavilions surmounting the tower is more successful, with those to the right all leaning to the right. These devices partially succeed in evoking the vertigo experienced when looking up at a high building, but they do damage the architectural solidity of the tower. The uppermost stage in particular appears as if it might gently flop over at any moment, bringing the statue crashing down.

The illustration was made to accompany a passage about the display of sculpture and, in the accompanying text in lecture 1, Turner did not discuss vertical convergence. Nevertheless, his representation of it in figure 92 seems deliberate. The diagram was intended to show the appearance of the elevated statue to a spectator at ground level, as part of an argument that sculptors should take full account of the position in which their sculptures will be displayed. Turner had to illustrate the statue's appearance from below, and a standard perspective representation, which could only have given this effect if viewed from its single fixed viewpoint, would clearly have been inappropriate for a large lecture audience. To reinforce the point the diagram was displayed alongside one in standard perspective (fig.20). This latter diagram uses a higher and more distant viewpoint – one of the things that treatises recommended to avoid problems when depicting high objects – and is clearly much less successful at representing height. Turner similarly employed dramatically but inconsistently sloping verticals in his diagrams of Pulteney Bridge (figs.48–9). However, as with St George's, Bloomsbury, these pictures were not primarily intended to illustrate an account of vertical convergence in the lectures.[55]

In work not connected with his perspective lectures, Turner sometimes represented vertical convergence by simply sloping verticals slightly to the left or to the right. This can be seen in a study of part of the portico of St Peter's (fig.96). In studies made in front of the motif, verticals occasionally lean consistently away from the viewpoint; but a view of the Grand Canal (fig.93) is more typical: some of the pencil drawing of the Palazzo Balbi in the left foreground leans to the right, but other verticals in watercolour incline to the left. Watercolour brushwork fails to keep to the same direction as pencil drawing in numerous other works. There is even less direct representation of vertical convergence in Turner's more highly finished works. (Indeed, in his early architectural works he often ruled vertical guidelines to ensure that his verticals stayed that way.) Although he gently sloped the uprights in many of his exhibited oil paintings, such as 'Regulus' (fig.87) and 'The Decline of the Carthaginian Empire' (fig.108), there is again no consistency in the way in which the verticals slope – some lean to the left, others to the right, while some are as vertical as any draughtsman could make them.

When he directly represented vertical convergence Turner simply avoided strict perpendiculars. He did not replace standard perspective with a consistent alternative geometrical system. In fact, for all his theoretical discussion of vertical convergence in his lectures, Turner directly depicted it less than many other artists. For example, a dissection with ruler and set-square of Claude's 'Seaport: The Embarkation of St Ursula' (fig.109) reveals more converging verticals than in either figure 108 or 'Dido Building Carthage' (B&J 131), Turner's 'pendant' to the Claude.[56]

'Only One Horizontal in Nature'

In his lectures Turner also criticised the failure of standard perspective to directly represent lateral convergence, a horizontal equivalent to vertical convergence. In 1811, towards the end of his second lecture, he explained the phenomenon. He displayed a large watercolour of the upper part of the Great Room at Somerset House (fig.94) – the room in which he lectured. The far wall is parallel to the picture plane and so, following the principles of standard perspective, its main horizontal architectural elements are represented by lines that are parallel to each other and to the horizon.[57] They do not converge on the picture surface. But Turner argued that the picture is wrong. Perhaps pointing up at the ceiling as he spoke, he observed: 'No line is parallel in nature but the [horizon]. The upper line of cornice to all those seated in [the] centre appears to dip each way, and the underneath part or lines appear to approach each other as they recede from the eye, looking at them from the centre.'[58] That is, only the horizon appears absolutely horizontal, and the horizontal lines of the architecture appear to converge together laterally as they get further from the spectator. Turner conceded that from a large enough distance the cornice 'appears straight', but insisted that however large the distance, the separate parts of each architectural element do still appear to converge: 'But even then, the underneath parts of the projections, or lines, approach towards each [other] as they recede from the eye.'[59] As with vertical convergence, standard perspective does not directly represent this lateral convergence on the picture surface.[60]

A rare example of Turner's direct representation of lateral convergence is his unfinished watercolour of the interior of Christ Church Cathedral, Oxford (fig.95). The parallel lines that represent the horizontal elements of the lower parts of the choir screen and transept show that these parts of the cathedral were parallel to the picture plane. Consistent with this, the nave is shown perpendicular to the picture plane: lines representing its upper parts converge to the perspective centre point, which is located just to the right of the bottom of the pulpit. (There is a small hole in the picture surface here, which probably resulted from Turner ruling lines to this point representing the walls of the nave.) The floor is not drawn so accurately, but it is consistent with the building being parallel and perpendicular to the picture plane and a viewpoint at the right-hand edge. So far, everything conforms to the rules of standard perspective. However, if the upper part of the arch between the nave and the crossing is considered, it will be seen that it includes a line that slopes downwards to the left.

fig.94 'Interior of the Great Room at Somerset House', lecture diagram 26 c.1810

Turner treated the higher horizontals of the north transept in the same way. But these elements of the building are parallel to the picture plane and so in standard perspective would be represented by horizontal lines. Turner broke the rules to give a greater sense of height and drama.

Turner did not depict lateral convergence in a consistent way. In one of the lecture diagams of St George's, Bloomsbury (fig.92) the top of the front face of the church tower slopes, representing the lateral convergence that standard perspective would ignore. The horizontal lines of the upper pavilions of the tower also slope, but unevenly, and less steeply than those of the top of the tower. Together with the indecisive vertical convergence, noted above, this lack of consistency creates the rather uncomfortable instability of the building.

fig.95 'Interior of Christ Church Cathedral, Oxford' c.1799

It is difficult to identify depictions of lateral convergence. This is demonstrated by a watercolour of part of the portico of St Peter's (fig.96) in which the downward slope of the high horizontals appears similar to that in the interior of Christ Church Cathedral (fig.95). The artist was positioned on the lower of the steps, which are perpendicular to the picture plane. However, at St Peter's itself the steps are not exactly perpendicular to the facade of the building. Therefore, the facade actually was not parallel to the picture plane and, in particular, its high horizontals were oblique to it. Thus, in standard perspective they should indeed slope downwards. Turner exploited the relationship between the steps and the portico to suggest lateral convergence without breaking the standard rules.

There seem to be very few other works in which Turner showed (or

fig.96 'The Portico of St Peter's, Rome' 1819

alluded to) lateral convergence. His general softening of the surface grid of parallel perspective owes more to a straightforward antipathy to accurately ruled lines than to any fully developed alternative theory of representation. Set against the forceful rejection of standard perspective in his lectures, his failure to take full account of vertical and lateral convergence in practice may be disappointing; but in view of his suspicion of theoretical systems it is not all that surprising.

Turner's Welcoming Foregrounds

When viewing many of Turner's paintings, we feel close to the scene being depicted, almost as if a single step forwards would take us into the picture space, like Alice passing through the looking glass. In part, this is because the foregrounds are large. Consider for example, 'The Parting of Hero and Leander' (fig.97): although the protagonists embrace at the centre of the picture, the strong perspective recession of the staircase firmly locates us to one side. We stand just to the left of the landscape painting that is set into the floor.[61] The foreground terrace is extremely large in scale compared to the rest of the scene; this means it is very close to us as we view the picture. Turner also produced relatively large foregrounds in much smaller pictures, for example 'Isola Bella, Lago Maggiore' (fig.98), a design for an illustration for the 1830 edition of Samuel Rogers's poem *Italy*. The balustrade at the right is so close that it almost passes out of the picture and into the space that the viewer occupies.[62]

To achieve these effects Turner placed the viewpoint very close to the picture surface. A short viewing distance widens the angle of view, allowing the picture to include more of the edges of the scene. In particular, it incorporates close but peripheral objects (see fig.99). Perspective theorists warned that this could lead to problematic distortion, but Turner brilliantly exploited its potential. A viewpoint close to the picture surface allows 'Ely Cathedral – The Interior of the Octagon' (fig.66) to include both the north and south piers where the nave meets the crossing. This work also encompasses a large vertical angle of view – a further effect of a short viewing distance (fig.100). In combination with its upright format, this allows the great height of the crossing to be depicted much more fully than would have been the case with a longer distance.[63]

Turner also used short viewing distances in order to devote a large

PAINTER OF PERSPECTIVE

fig.97 'The Parting of Hero and Leander' exh.1837

fig.98 'Isola Bella, Lago Maggiore' 1827

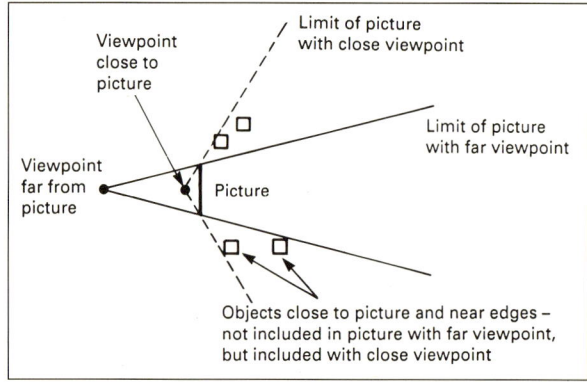

fig.99 The effect of a close viewpoint and wide viewing angle shown from above (modern diagram)

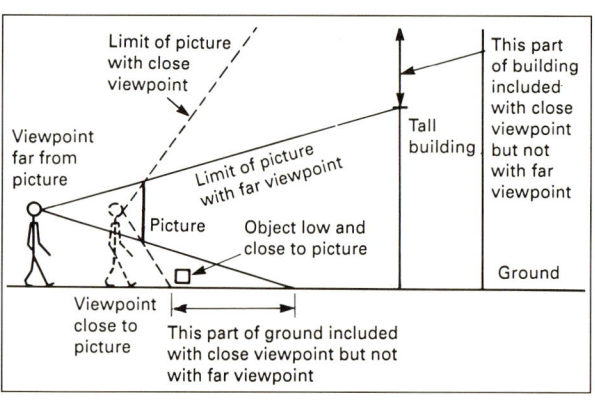

fig.100 The effect of a close viewpoint and wide viewing angle shown from one side (modern diagram)

[78]

area of the picture surface to the floor. In this case, the part of the foreground depicted just above a picture's bottom edge, would have been only a few feet from the artist's eye when he viewed the scene before him.[64] It therefore represents the continuation of the place where he stood. In standard perspective, spectators at the correct viewpoint have the same geometrical relationship to the picture that the artist did and so, in a painting such as 'The Parting of Hero and Leander' (fig.97), the large, close floor is precisely the one on which viewers themselves must be standing when viewing the picture.[65]

This also explains the scale of some of the objects in Turner's foregrounds: they are large because they are so near. As we look beyond the waving figures towards Hero and Leander we are aware of an area much closer to us. There are objects to the right of the viewing position, just cropped by the bottom of the picture. They have such presence that we almost feel that we could reach down and touch them. The immediate foreground sometimes includes items that could have been simply left on the ground when the artist (or the viewer) took a step backwards to survey the scene. There may be a self-referential palette and brushes (fig.114), or perhaps some refreshments and a chair that seem to await the artist's return (fig.121).

Turner regularly specified the exact spot where viewers sit or stand. In early work the paving on which he stood as he made the sketch may be shown in the foreground (fig.101). He continued to employ this subtle but effective compositional device throughout his life; for example, in one of his last on-the-spot views of the coast of Europe (fig.102).[66] In

fig.101 'Mountains beside a Lake' 1802

fig.102 'White Cliffs, Eu' 1845

fig.103 'Naples with Vesuvius' 1819

fig.105 'Forum Romanum, for Mr Soane's Museum' exh.1826

fig.104 'St Anne's Hill II (In the Garden)' c.1832

these works with large, close foregrounds perspective still functions as a view through a window, but viewers feel as if their noses are pressed on the glass as they look not only from side to side, but can see downwards, too, almost glimpsing their own feet.

If neo-classical history painters often provided a stage on which characters performed their significant action, then Turner does this for his spectators: his use of perspective invites participation in the performance.[67] His indications of a 'viewing stage' can be quite subtle; it may be the edge of the terrace on which he stood (fig.103), or the bench on which he knelt (fig.104). Sometimes, the stage is not directly shown, but is indicated by what may be regarded as the proscenium

fig.106 'Rouen Cathedral' c.1832

fig.107 'Lausanne, Looking East' 1841

fig.108 'The Decline of the Carthaginian Empire' exh.1817

fig.109 Claude Lorrain, 'Seaport: The Embarkation of St Ursula' 1641

arch: subtle framing at the top of the picture firmly connects the viewer's position to the picture space. Turner employed this device in both large works like 'Forum Romanum' (fig.105) and smaller ones like the view of Rouen Cathedral that was engraved for his *Annual Tour* of 1834 (fig.106). In some the viewpoint is beneath a bridge, perhaps in a boat, or below an arched trellis (fig.104). Note, however, that in some works, the framing arch lies between the main parts of the scene depicted and the spectator's own space, separating rather than connecting the two. Arches well within the picture space can also serve to keep the viewer away from the middleground and background, depending on the availability of routes that can be followed within the picture space to reach the middleground.[68]

Even pictures made from high above a distant scene often indicate Turner's (and hence a viewer's) position, such as the wall on which he stood to obtain a better view of the city below (fig.107). Many of Turner's Claudian landscapes have an extensive view over the background, but their foregrounds are much closer to the viewer, with lower viewpoints, than in Claude's paintings. Turner negated the sense of ownership and control of land that Claude offered his viewers.[69]

'The Decline of the Carthaginian Empire' (fig.108) benefits from the full potential of a short distance between artist/spectator and picture surface. There is a much stronger relationship between the viewer and the picture than in a Claude seaport (fig.109). In Turner's picture the viewpoint is to the left of the centre, above a slightly raised platform on which viewers stand to survey the scene. At their feet lie objects cast aside, including a tambourine. Further 'debris' fills the bottom centre

of the foreground. The relative closeness of the floor and these objects is denoted by their large scale in comparison with, for example, that of the nearest figures. The spectator's sense of proximity to the picture space is further enhanced by the way in which the nearest part of the lower step fills the right-hand side of the field of vision. The architecture at the left-hand side and the more distant concave of the edge of the port also contribute to the ability of the picture to fully occupy the viewer's visual attention. The building's proximity removes any need to look beyond it at the left-hand margin. The central curve has been used to pull the extreme right-hand part of the foreground round, towards the centre of the picture. This widens the scene that the picture is able to encompass. Even if the close viewing position remained, the sense of engagement would be much reduced if the curve were straightened, the steps differently positioned, the viewing stage or debris omitted, or the framing building removed.

fig.110 'Town on the Loire' c.1832

This shows that it is not only the perspective geometry that determines the relationship between the viewer and the picture space: the artist's choice of motif is important, too. Turner sometimes depicted scenes, particularly roads or bridges, that widened as they approached the picture, thereby further increasing the size of the foreground and its ability to embrace the spectator (fig.110). His most daring scenes are perhaps those which curved as they approached him (fig.111), allowing him to break down some of the rectilinearity of standard perspective without necessarily breaking its rules. But it can be impossible to determine how much is contributed by the shape of the motif itself, by the closeness of the viewpoint, or perhaps by the deliberate curving of forms.

fig.111 'Saumur' c.1832

Rejecting Rectilinearity

Pictures which strictly follow the rules of standard linear perspective are usually dominated by straight lines. All lines that are straight in life, however far from the centre of view they may be, and at whatever angle to the picture plane, are depicted by straight lines on the picture surface. Standard perspective is directly based on the premise that rays of light travel from objects to the eye without curving and are intersected by a plane surface. The picture surface is normally not only flat, but rectangular in shape, adding to the dominance of straight lines.

This rigorous rectilinearity suits architectural draughtsmen and history painters. The former can exploit it to strengthen the solidity and structure of buildings, and the latter to create a classical, unified, stable rectangular framework in which significant action can take place.

But Turner was primarily a landscape painter. As Ruskin wrote: 'That all forms of acknowledged beauty are composed exclusively of curves will, I believe, be at once allowed ... [There is] subtlety and constancy of curvature in all natural forms whatsoever.' After listing a few exceptions to this (including rays of light themselves), he continued: 'For the most part the eye is fed in natural forms with a grace of curvature which no hand nor instrument can follow.'[70] Turner shared this view: 'The meandering river and the rushing cataract appear sometimes not wholly unapplicable [to perspective], but they evade such weak control – turning aside like graceful elegance, defying all rules.' He also likened perspective to 'the gossamer down – a web too weak to hold ... the forms of muscular exertion [and] unable to assume the flowing, undulating forms of female beauty.'[71] Indeed 'though some forms appear amenable to geometric laws, yet upon the application of rules strictly speaking they turn aside with graceful elegance from all rules and decline the comparison and restraint.'[72] Turner developed the above passages from one in Thomas Malton's *Compleat Treatise on Perspective*, where it is argued that this is not a failing of perspective because 'irregular curved figures or objects but seldom occur in practice'.[73]

Turner did not agree: 'irregular curved' forms may not have occurred often in Malton's practice, but landscape is dominated by them. Furthermore, the experience of vision is very different to the fixed Euclidian geometry of standard perspective. As shown above, to better represent the breadth of nature and vision, Turner sometimes deployed wide, close foregrounds and multiple directions of recession; and he softened some of perspective's rectilinearity by avoiding ruled lines. Even if treated with suspicion by many perspective theorists, these manipulations are just within the bounds of standard perspective and so do not amount to a full-scale rejection of it. But Turner held many doubts about standard perspective and in the latter part of his second perspective lecture, examined many of its problems. Parts of that discussion, such as those about marginal distortion and lateral convergence, have been examined above, but here it is necessary to present some further sections. Much of the material is not fully resolved and amounts to little more than a series of questions, rather than answers; but it is clear that Turner firmly and consistently argued that standard perspective is, putting it a little bluntly, too straight.

For example, he considered a footnote from Malton that ridicules a suggestion that light may be reflected in 'a regular parabolic kind of curve'. However, far from sharing Malton's rejection of the concept, Turner first raised its status by attributing it directly to Newton, and then developed it much further by speculating that if 'incurvation of the ray of light ... is admissable in crystalline bodies [i.e. during reflection], may not our vision receive every impression on the like parabolide curve?'[74] That is, Turner proposed that light may travel from objects to the eye in curved lines, rather than straight ones. This is a remarkable comment as no similar suggestion is made in any British eighteenth- or early nineteenth-century perspective treatise. As Malton affirmed: 'That vision is conveyed in right lines to the eye I presume no person will attempt to dispute ... I shall therefore give it as a general axiom.'[75]

In the discussion that followed in lecture 2 Turner spoke of the difficulties of depicting objects that 'increase by the part perspectively, whereas in vision they diminish in ratio to the circle of vision.'[76] Further:

> The eye must take in all objects upon a parabolic curve. For in looking into space the eye cannot but receive only what is within its limits of extended sight, what must form a circle to the eye. Therefore, as it always must view only part of that circle at a time, the objects must be thrown on a part of a circle instead of a square. And as every line is more or less elevated, so it must partake of a parabolic curve.[77]

Already alarmed by Turner's premise that standard perspective fails to take account of the curving nature of human visual experience and distorts the visual world, his lecture audience cannot have been helped greatly by somewhat obscure suggestions such as: 'as every line is more or less elevated so it must partake of a parabolic curve'; or: 'may not our vision receive every impression on the ... parabolide curve?' To be fair, Turner did write more at other points in the lectures (although probably not for the 1811 course), but none of his musings amount to a fully codified alternative means of representation, such as those later proposed by Parsey and Herdman in the 1830s and 1840s.[78] Turner did not propose a new system because he distrusted all systems, arguing that however comprehensive a theory claimed to be there would inevitably be circumstances in which it would fail. For example, he doubted that rules could be laid down for the way in which light may curve, because there would always be circumstances in which 'the said rules would not give the object'.[79]

It is, therefore, perhaps not surprising that Turner did not consistently curve straight lines in his pictures; those examples that can be found seem to have been arrived at pragmatically, on a one-off basis.[80] Furthermore, these are normally less radical than his lecture pronouncements would seem to suggest. In fact the majority of his architectural forms follow the rules of standard perspective. However, on occasion he did break free of standard perspective's rectilinear rigour, deliberately curving lines that it would render straight, and even twisting space itself.

'Rome from the Vatican'

'Rome from the Vatican' (fig.112) is generally seen as marking a crucial stage in Turner's career. The huge painting, whose full exhibited title was 'Rome, from the Vatican. Raffaelle, Accompanied by La Fornarina, Preparing his Pictures for the Decoration of the Loggia', was the only one that Turner exhibited at the Royal Academy in 1820, following his first visit to Italy, and coinciding with the tercentenary of Raphael's death. It contains several anachronisms, and the space that Turner constructed in this picture has been seen as unsuccessful, perhaps the result of hasty planning.[81] I hope to demonstrate that the picture space is not the product of rushed thinking. Rather, it was produced with care and can be regarded as one of Turner's main public statements about alternatives to standard perspective.

The foreground represents Pope Leo X's private loggia on the second floor of the Pontifical Palace in the Vatican. The ceiling is painted with biblical narratives and decorative motifs, including ambitious perspective illusions, by Raphael and his many assistants, who completed work there by 1519.[82] The viewpoint is from the third bay, which illustrates the story of Noah; to the right the end of the loggia includes an empty plinth. The centre of the picture is a view over Piazza Santa Pietro to the city of Rome, with the Apennine mountains in the distance. To the left of this view, and across a courtyard from the loggia, is a further part of the Pontifical Palace. The horizontals of the right-hand side of this building nearly all converge to a single viewpoint, on approximately the same level as the distant horizon. The recession of the right-hand bays of the loggia is not so precise, but is based on the same horizon height, indicating immediately that the picture has at least some spatial coherence.[83] But questions do arise: What is the architectural element filling the picture's left-hand edge? Why is the arch at the top of the picture so large? What happens to the balustrade of the loggia after it passes behind the figures? And why are the figures so small?

PAINTER OF PERSPECTIVE

Answers can be sought in Turner's preliminary studies. The *Tivoli and Rome* sketchbook contains several sketches of the loggia, including details of its decoration and a view along to one end, made from a position close to the inside wall of the fourth bay (fig.113). As the viewpoint is quite low, there is no distant view out through the arches. There are strong similarities between the right-hand half of this sketch and the right-hand third of the painting. The *Rome C[olour] Studies* sketchbook contains a further study, probably also made on the spot (fig.114).[84] For this, Turner chose a higher viewpoint (at about the same height as the top of the blank doorway containing the plinth – here crowned with its bust of Raphael), close to the balustrade to enable the

fig.112 'Rome from the Vatican. Raffaelle, Accompanied by La Fornarina, Preparing his Pictures for the Decoration of the Loggia' exh.1820

fig.114 Study for 'Rome from the Vatican' 1819

fig.113 *Tivoli and Rome* sketchbook, Study for 'Rome from the Vatican' 1819

PAINTER OF PERSPECTIVE

inclusion of an extensive view out from the loggia. It is not possible to be certain which bay of the loggia is represented in this sketch as the nearest pillar blocks the view of any others that may lie behind it, but it seems to be quite close to the end.[85]

Many elements of the scene in figure 114, although drawn freehand, conform with standard perspective; but, significantly, the balustrade is not represented by a straight line. It bends at the right of the palette and brushes that rest on it (and allude to Turner's – and Raphael's – presence in the loggia). Also, it makes a rather sharp turn where it meets the pillar of the loggia – continued in a straight line, it would miss the pillar, and intercept the leaning figure.

The bent balustrade results from a spatial twist: the front face of the section of the palace in the middle-distance at the left-hand side of the sketch is actually parallel to the loggia (see fig.115). Thus, in standard perspective, the balustrade, and the loggia itself, would run across horizontally and be aligned with the palace building and the bottom of the picture. Instead, Turner rotated the right-hand part of the loggia through almost ninety degrees. Immediately to the left of the front pillar of the loggia Turner correctly showed the front wall of the

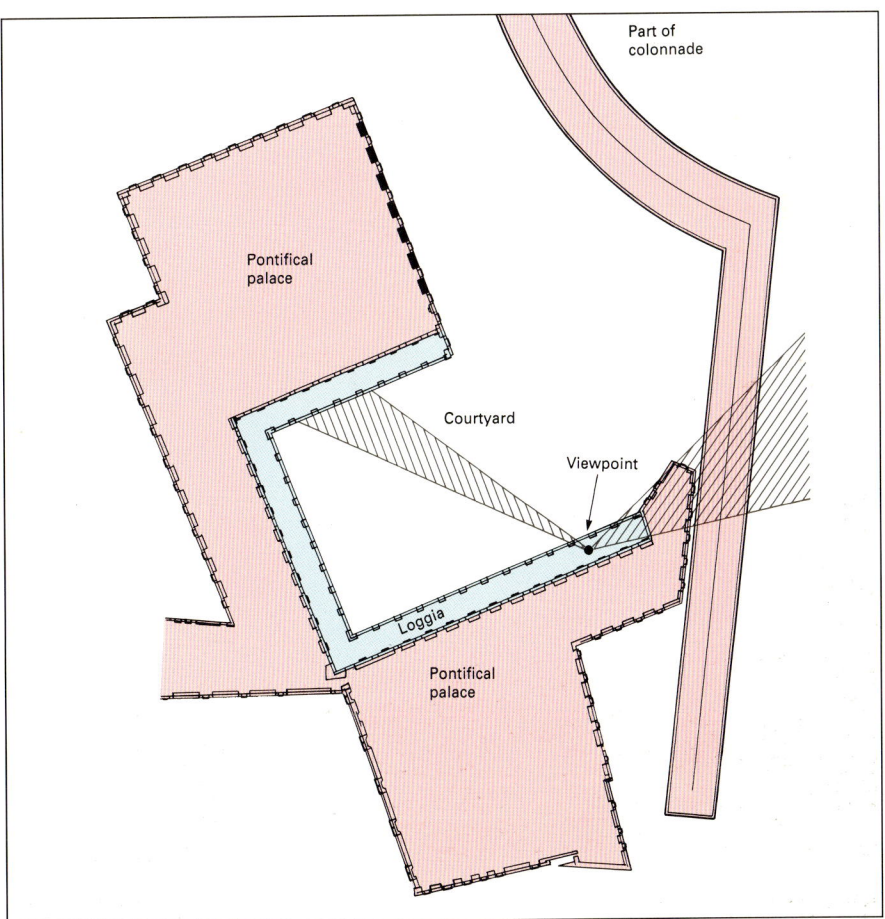

fig.115 Plan of the Vatican. The viewpoint used for fig.112 is shown, together with the limits of the view encompassed in the painting. (The hatched area represents those parts of the distant view obscured by the architecture of the loggia.) (Modern diagram)

[87]

building angled forward in front of the loggia (see fig.115). This was carefully preserved in the painting, the central region of which has many similarities to this study.

The space of the finished painting (fig.112) is largely the product of the skilful combination of the two studies. The angle of the loggia at the right-hand side of the painting is about midway between its positions in the two sketches. The artist's position was slightly nearer the balustrade than the one used for figure 113, but further back than that of figure 114. The viewpoint is to the left of the picture, roughly aligned with the artist's palette.[86] For the painting Turner extended the scene at the left; in fact the object that closes that side is a frontal view of the inside of the left-hand pillar of the loggia's third bay. The original pillar is of course actually aligned with the rest of the loggia, but Turner showed it at a quite different angle.

Turner's greatest spatial stroke was in the top centre of the picture, where he bent the arch at the front of the third bay through an angle of perhaps forty-five degrees so that it would be able to meet the top of the left-most pillar, but beyond the top edge of the picture. The floor of the loggia, too, must turn in order to align with the bottom edge of the picture at the left-hand margin. Thus, Turner made it shoot forwards, rapidly increasing in size, but deftly cut it off with the bottom edge of the picture just at the moment a distracting curve would otherwise have to have been depicted.

Turner's twists and turns do much more than simply reconcile differently angled parts of the loggia – they help to incorporate the viewer in the picture space. After the arch leaves the top of the picture, it soars off the picture surface and over the viewer's head, 'like the Milky Way', in the words of one late nineteenth-century commentator.[87] Below, the implied floor shoots round pulling the viewer into the loggia. There is no need to take even a single step forward to enter the picture space: anyone viewing the picture from nearby already stands in the loggia itself. If the picture is viewed from a close point, the receding loggia occupies the right-hand side of the visual field and the nearest and largest pillar of the loggia fills the left; above the painted vault must arch, and beneath the marble floor must run. The picture is all-embracing. As the picture space was not constructed according to a precise geometrical system it is not appropriate to specify an exact viewing distance. However, the picture needs to be viewed from closer than about three feet if it is to fill the visual field when viewed with one eye.[88]

The height of the viewpoint can be given more exactly. It is level with the top of the segmental pediment over the plinth, higher in the loggia than that of either of the sketches – it was necessary to raise the horizon to preserve the view in figure 114 while retreating back from the balustrade. This height places the spectator not directly on the loggia floor, but above it, standing on the carpet-covered table, which provides a viewing platform. The picture should therefore be hung quite low, to enable viewers to see the picture from this height.

The table is a crucial element of the composition. Firstly, it aids the transition from the centre to the left by means of the carefully chosen angles of recession of its sides, which link the two sides of the picture better than a twisting floor ever could. Secondly, it partially obviates the need to depict the left-hand section of the balustrade, which would otherwise have to curve round dramatically to meet the left-hand pillar. Were it to continue to the left-hand side, the balustrade would meet the pillar well above the top of the palette. It would increase substantially in size and dominate the picture. Turner adapted the decoration of the pillar (omitting the horizontal band of decoration at the level of the top of the balustrade) to further disguise the fact that the balustrade is omitted. Note that the balustrade is rather unresolved and changes height and direction awkwardly on either side of La Fornarina. However, further to the left Turner treated it with great suavity: he did not show it at all to the left of the tondo of the Madonna. Instead, to the right of the head of the statue, he picked up the line of the balustrade with the colonnades far below in the piazza, aiding the transition with the circular form of the tondo. This piece of perspectival wit also produces a substantial curve on the picture surface that balances that of the arch at the top.

fig.116 *Tivoli and Rome* sketchbook, Study for 'Rome from the Vatican' 1819

The table plays a further role. As well as locating the viewer, it acts as a stage on which Raphael, accompanied by La Fornarina, can arrange his pictures. Things on the stage are undoubtedly depicted at a much smaller scale than other parts of the picture, and La Fornarina is significantly smaller than Raphael. Their diminutive scale can be appreciated if the painting is compared to a related study (fig.116), in which the relative sizes of the figures are much less problematical. The architecture twists in this work, but much less dramatically.[89] In the oil the figures clearly do not fit spatially. Furthermore, Raphael had died long before the piazza colonnades were built, so the figures do not fit temporally either.[90]

However, apart from the figures, and items directly associated with them, the architectural and landscape elements are spatially coherent, although based on material gathered from different viewpoints. As in almost all Turner's pictures, there is a single viewpoint from which all elements make sense. Turner took great pains to ensure that this was so. For example, the right-hand side of the largest pillar can just be seen because it is perpendicular to the picture plane and the viewpoint is just to the right of it. With similar care, Turner took account of the fact that he had shown the palace building opposite with its front face turned slightly towards the picture plane. So, although the building is further to the right than the left-most pillar, more of the building's right-hand face can be seen. Other details throughout the picture were as carefully thought out to ensure that, even though an alternative to standard perspective has been employed, there is still a single viewpoint. In his lectures Turner argued that one of the benefits of a thorough knowledge of perspective was that it gave artists the ability to manipulate the viewpoints from which they showed objects in their pictures, a skill with which he was brilliantly conversant.

The picture space of 'Rome from the Vatican' is unusual, but it is not unique. About two years after completing it, Turner followed George IV's first state visit to Edinburgh, an event organised by Sir Walter Scott.[91] On Sunday 25 August 1822 the King attended St Giles's Cathedral. Turner made two pencil studies of the interior, both taken from near the bottom of the pulpit, although apparently not during the service itself. For one of these he positioned himself at the edge of the nave (fig.117), but for the other he stood in an aisle (fig.118) and drew the scene before him with the same twists in the picture space that he had used in 'Rome from the Vatican'. He retained this arrangement for his oil painting which includes the King and congregation (fig.119), curving the vault of the aisle over the viewing position, and extending the aisle floor out of the bottom of the picture, again cropping it just at the stage where it would need to begin to curve.

fig.117 *King's Visit to Edinburgh* sketchbook, Study for 'George IV at St Giles's, Edinburgh' 1822

fig.118 *King's Visit to Edinburgh* sketchbook, Study for 'George IV at St Giles's, Edinburgh' 1822

fig.119 'George IV at St Giles's, Edinburgh' c.1822

In 'George IV at St Giles's, Edinburgh' the rest of the foreground is also treated in a similar way to that of 'Rome from the Vatican'. The place of the balustrade is taken by the ends of the box pews which terminate exactly where they would otherwise have to rise up awkwardly. Turner cleverly disguised the potentially problematic floor in this area by carefully positioning a large cushion that supports two women wearing long, trailing dresses. With great compositional skill and wit, the cushion is circular; this both aids the transition between the end of the pews and the columns at the far left, and also alludes to the curving perspective in the vicinity. In a similar vein, Turner ended the corner of the pews with a compositionally important concave curve, and included a rounded table. The picture omits a potentially difficult railing that he hesitantly included in the sketch (fig.118). The only spatial uncertainty in this area is the right-hand side of the base of the column which uncomfortably changes direction just above the bottom of the picture.

'George IV at St Giles's, Edinburgh' is much smaller than 'Rome from the Vatican' and so could never be as all-embracing visually, even to someone very close to the picture. Nevertheless, if viewed from near its left-hand edge at a height slightly above the heads of the standing figures, a convincing spatial effect is experienced. In the centre, the pulpit canopy (based on that in the alternative interior sketch – fig.117) sets up a strong relationship between the relatively humble preacher and the opulently attired King, to whom the viewer's attention is also drawn by the burst of bright light high in the nave. Again, at the peripheries of the scene, the aisle recedes to the right and blocks further views to the left.

By curving the foreground architecture in 'Rome from the Vatican' and 'George IV at St Giles's, Edinburgh', Turner broke the window of standard perspective to allow the viewer to enter the picture space.

'The Limits of Extended Sight': Petworth Park

Turner not only experimented with curving architecture, he also twisted the earth itself in an attempt to produce scenes similar in extent to those experienced when directly viewing a landscape. He noted that views extend from the spectator in all directions. Thus the limit of the full field of vision is a complete circle, right around the body. At any specific moment the spectator sees segments of this circle. Turner

fig.124 *Petworth* sketchbook, 'Petworth Park' *c.*1827

fig.125 'Petworth Park' (detail) *c.*1827

explained to his lecture audience: 'The theory of vision is to take into view comparatively all objects. The eye can only be said but to receive portions of an extended sight ... which must form an entire circle. Therefore it must always view but a part of that circle at a time.' If 'the limits of extended sight ... form an entire circle', what should artists do? In theory, they could produce circular pictures: 'Why should [objects] not be thrown on part of a circle commensurate to [the] angle of vision, instead of a square?'[92] This is partly a reference to panoramic paintings, which were common in early nineteenth-century London. These vast pictures, usually housed in specially designed buildings, linked consecutive views together on a curved surface and surrounded the spectator on all sides. Turner explained that they replicated the circle of view: 'The eye is within the area of its circle. This is the case in nature [and] in panoramic views, and they are produced by such means.'[93]

However, Turner never produced a panorama. In fact he never even used a curved picture surface. He did consider transferring the image from a panorama to a flat canvas, but concluded that this would be unacceptable because the resulting picture would have multiple viewpoints. This is shown in a sketch in which he 'unwrapped' a panorama (fig.120). He wanted to preserve, as far as possible, the single viewpoint of standard perspective and so had to find other solutions.

'Petworth Park: Tillington Church in the Distance' (fig.121 on p.94) is one of Turner's most successful creations of a wide all-embracing

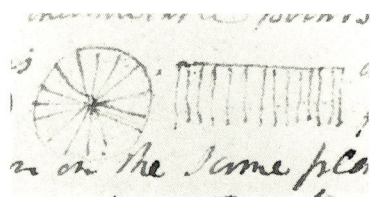

fig.120 Sketch of geometry of a panorama in endpapers of Turner's copy of Joseph Priestley, *A Familiar Introduction to the Theory and Practice of Perspective*, 1770, *c.*1809–28

fig.126 *Petworth* sketchbook 'Petworth Park' c.1827

view on a conventional, flat picture surface. He painted it in c.1828, possibly as a study for a work designed to hang in Petworth House itself.[94] The landscape is extensive and broad and does not appear to be restricted by the edges of the canvas. At the sides it seems possible to see parts of the park that would be hidden by the frame in a more conventional picture. In the centre, the ground bends downwards, made concave by the sun, increasing the distance to the horizon. This dip also contributes to the curved feeling of the foreground. Indeed, the entire landscape curves around the central sun. The sun breaks the straight line of the horizon; and the clouds arch above it. At the right, shadows of deer radiate from it; at the left, dogs running to their master align with it. Even the paving of the terrace and the tops of the trees seem, focused on the sun.

The curving of the foreground is reinforced by a path that lies between the terrace and the grass. Turner shows it more clearly in some of his studies (figs.122–3 on p.94). The path is a crucial element of the foreground composition: it counteracts the sharply angled foreground terrace which would otherwise lead the eye below the picture's bottom edge. At the lower right of the oil, after sweeping the eye back onto the canvas, it sharply changes direction to pull the edges of the view inwards. It also contributed to the tight curves at the sides of the picture, as other sketches show (figs.124–6).

Turner positioned the terrace extremely carefully. Its angle allows it to interact perfectly with the path and it is cropped at exactly the right point – any longer and it would have had to begin to curve upwards. At the other side, distortions in the paving are disguised by the chair and bottle. As in 'Rome from the Vatican' and 'George IV at St Giles's', Turner concealed those places where he would have had to break standard perspective rules too flagrantly. He achieved an effect of curved space without explicitly representing as curved any lines that would normally be depicted as straight. The rectilinear terrace and the

fig.121 'Petworth Park: Tillington Church in the Distance' c.1828

fig.122 'Sunset across Petworth Park' 1827

fig.123 'Petworth Park: Sunset with a Cart' 1827

resolutely vertical window frame at the left-hand side help stabilise the landscape and prevent it spinning or shifting. They also locate the viewing position near to the left, a location reinforced by the large scale of the foreground objects at that side.

With its combination of straight and curving lines, the composition is a little like a wheel. The shadows, dogs and lines of paving radiate like spokes from the sun at the hub, with the path and the arching clouds forming the rim. The surface geometry is like Turner's diagram of a panorama (fig.120), with a central eye looking in many directions. This is of course coincidental, but the picture is an attempt to squeeze a wide, even 'panoramic', view into a rectangular format. The

fig.127 'Glade and Greensward' 1827

broad scope of the painting can be appreciated by comparing it to distant views of the park in Turner's *Petworth* sketchbook. The background of the painting incorporates material collected on no less than three landscape-format pages: the full compass of one double-page sketch (fig.124), together with the left-hand page of another (fig.126, see pp.92–3). Although the oil is itself wide, its relative width is less than half that of the total of the three sketchbook pages.[95] Thus, Turner had to compress the view to incorporate it all, and curved the foreground as he did so. Further studies of the view from the house include many other elements of the final painting, such as animals with shadows radiating from a central sun. The animals in one study (fig.127) may have suggested the line of dogs. In another (fig.123), cattle pulling a cart cast long shadows as they follow the path – and perform a similar function to the deer of the oil. If this latter study is placed alongside another view from the house (fig.122), the scene encompassed is about the same extent in width as that in the oil, allowing for an overlap in the centre, The angle of the terrace at the left of the oil and the curve of the path at the right seem to owe much to these two views, each of which was taken in a different direction.

Yet further studies may have contributed to Turner's thinking about the picture space, and it is not possible to be certain which studies were made in front of the motif, which are compositional studies and which were intended as completely independent works.[96] However, it is clear that in 'Petworth Park: Tillington Church in the Distance' Turner combined several views originally made from a variety of points into a single image, and exploited curving motifs in the park itself, together with other observed and imagined elements, to give a remarkably wide, even panoramic, scene that is coherent from a single viewpoint and on a conventional flat rectangular canvas.

The extreme curves of the picture space of 'Petworth Park' are unusual, but in other works Turner used many of the individual elements that contributed to it. For example he regularly sketched distant landscapes (and sometimes townscapes, too) in a wide format. To do this he either used a full double-page spread in a sketchbook for a single scene, or divided pages into strips so that they could include more than one view. The width of such sketches can be up to ten times their height and in extreme cases on-the-spot studies can be five times wider than studio works based on them.[97] Much of the difference can be accounted for by larger skies and foregrounds in studio works, but views from sketches were often squeezed to change their format, and sometimes twisted in the process. Sometimes foregrounds curve up the sides of pictures in order to better incorporate the expansive, if compressed, middlegrounds and distances. Turner also curved scenes when he sketched directly from nature; examples include some of the pre-

fig.128 'A View on the Rhine or Neckar' 1840

paratory studies for 'Rome from the Vatican' and 'George IV at St Giles's' (figs.114, 118).

Turner regularly exploited the full potential of curved elements in the scenes before him. He concentrated on the curved edges of lakes, seas and rivers, and sometimes accentuated them by drawing tightly curved lines on the surface of the water (fig.128). Like the curves at the sides of 'Petworth Park', these lines pull the edges of the scene inwards and distract the eye from the picture's hard straight edges to give softer, more fluid bounds. Turner also enhanced the curves of the ground. He increased any convexity present in pastoral landscapes (fig.129), and rounded the edges where sublime mountain slopes meet valley floors. In extreme cases, he swept the ground up into a vortex of vapour or wind, dissolving the earth itself and swirling it into the air (figs.130–1).

fig.129 'Dinant from the South-East: Evening' c.1839

Turner used combinations of all these effects to avoid the narrow, hard-edged views of standard perspective and suggest the full extent of nature. Even his smallest pictures can engage viewers in broad, expansive, unrestrained landscapes that seem to extend far beyond the arbitrary limits set by the frame.

fig.130 'Goldau' c.1842

fig.131 After J.M.W. Turner, 'Loch Coriskin' 1834

Variant Views: Vortices and Vignettes

Turner's exploitation of vortices went further than the representation of distant storms and swirls of vapour. In the early 1840s he exhibited a series of paintings dominated by near-symmetrical frame-filling frontal vortices. They confront the right angles and straight edges of a conventional rectangular picture format, instead creating a circular composition. Like other works in the series, 'Shade and Darkness – The Evening of the Deluge' (fig.132) and 'Light and Colour (Goethe's Theory) – the Morning after the Deluge' (fig.133) are painted on square canvases to minimise the amount of picture surface left untouched by centralising curves. To intensify the effect they were originally exhibited with their corners covered, giving an almost octagonal picture boundary. In earlier works in the series Turner had gone further and used a completely circular frame.[98]

fig.132 'Shade and Darkness – The Evening of the Deluge' exh.1843

The way in which these circles round the bounds of the scene is firmly grounded in perspective theory. We have seen that in his lectures Turner argued that the full field of vision extends horizontally right around the viewer's head, in a circle. He also believed that the bounds of the field of view were circular in the vertical plane. The consequence of these two circular limits is that the full, three-dimensional field of view is a sphere, with the viewer at the centre. This idea was not uncommon when Turner wrote his lectures, but it was generally felt to be irrelevant to perspective – any suggestion that pictures may be better painted on spherical surfaces was rejected by perspective theorists who insisted that artists should always think in terms of a relatively narrow scene through a rectangular window.[99] Turner was broader in his outlook; as has been shown above, works such as 'Rome from the Vatican' and 'Petworth Park: Tillington Church in the Distance' are, in part, attempts to reconcile elements of the horizontal circle of view with a conventional flat picture surface.

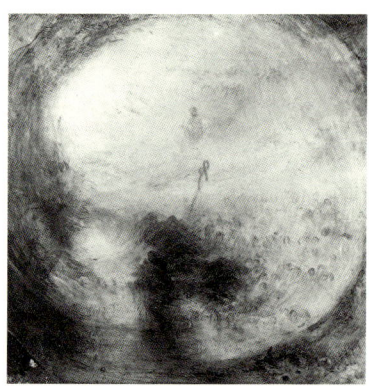

fig.133 'Light and Colour (Goethe's Theory) – The Morning after the Deluge – Moses Writing the Book of Genesis' exh.1843

Similarly, 'Shade and Darkness' and 'Light and Colour' can be seen as attempts to take account of the circular vertical limits of the field of view. Although Turner first wrote about the concept of the circular field of view in c.1810 and lectured for the last time in 1828, it was still being discussed when he began producing his 'circular' paintings, c.1840. No lesser a critic than John Ruskin explored it in a series of papers published in the *Architectural Magazine* of 1838–9 and, rather incongruously, the 1840 edition of Humphry Repton's *Landscape Gardening and Landscape Architecture*. Ruskin, writing under the pseudonym Kata Phusin, concluded (quite erroneously) that the eye cannot see objects further than thirty degrees from its central axis. Thus, 'the limit [of vision] is a circle, whose diameter subtends sixty degrees, whose centre is opposite the eye, and whose area is a section of the cone of rays by which the landscape is made sensible to the eye.'[100] He noted that this line of argument could be taken to imply that pictures should be circular. However, for a host of reasons, both practical and compositional, as well as theoretical, rectangular pictures were undoubtedly preferable. But Ruskin insisted that the circular sixty-degree field of view could not be ignored by artists. So, at great length, and with some confusion, he calculated rules that would allow rectangular pictures to take it into account (in fact he eventually settled on an elliptical limit, rather than an exactly circular one). Ruskin strictly specified the most appropriate proportion of height to width: 'The edge or frame of the picture ... is not an arbitrary enclosure of a certain number of touches ... nor is it to be extended or diminished as the artist wishes to include more or fewer objects ... its size and form are ... regulated by laws of perspective as distinct and inviolable.'[101] Like generations of perspective theorists before him, Ruskin insisted that pictures should be based strictly around a single fixed perspective viewpoint, and laid down precise rules about viewing distances.

Ruskin's prescriptions about picture formats are ridiculously impractical, and so cannot have impressed Turner. However, Turner did discuss perspective with Ruskin,[102] and shared his belief in the circular limit of view (although not his limitation of it to a sixty-degree maximum). One particular part of Ruskin's argument seems to have contributed directly to Turner's series of 'circular' paintings. This concerns the treatment of the corners of pictures. Ruskin noted that even if artists followed his strict rules, corners would still be out of the circular/elliptical field of view. Thus, in terms of his theory, they 'might be vague and subdued in colour, and totally without objects.' However, 'this would draw too much attention to them, [so] the artist continues his proximate colour into them ... keeping his brush in circular sweeps, indicating the form of the ellipse [that bounds the field of view].'[103] This is exactly how Turner treats the corners of, for example, 'Light and Colour' (fig.133). Indeed, so marked is Turner's evocation of a circular bound in this latter work that it has been suggested that at one stage he intended it to have a circular frame, rather than the nearly octagonal one in which it was first exhibited.[104]

As a whole, Turner's series of 'circular' works explores means of incorporating a circular field of view. The first three took a direct approach and were simply exhibited in circular frames. For the next four (e.g. figs.132–3) Turner chose quasi-octagons (that is, squares with the corners obscured). In the final two, Turner came closest to Ruskin's preference. He adopted a conventional square format, but still painted the corners with curving brushstrokes (e.g. fig.134 on p.101).[105] However, Turner did not follow the instruction to keep the corners completely free of objects, and certainly did not share Ruskin's belief that the viewer literally could not see objects located more than thirty degrees from the eye's central axis.

Ruskin's idea was based on an assumption that the eye can only focus distinctly on a single point at a time. This is a question of the physiology of vision, a subject too complex to explore fully here.[106] A few of its implications (and complexities) can be appreciated by considering the varied interpretations of the optical aims of Turner's vignettes, often regarded as one of the key sources of the series of 'circular' paintings. Turner first produced these small works in the late 1820s. They were designed as book illustrations and, by definition, are unbounded, allowing the image to blend gently into the page. Although they can be placed in a tradition, Turner took the vignette form to new heights.[107] His first examples, such as those for the 1830 edition of Samuel Rogers's poem *Italy* are usually (although not invariably) broadly rectangular in format (e.g. fig.98), but later ones, such as those illustrating Scott's *Poetical Works* (1833–4), Rogers's *Poems* of 1834 (fig.135) and an 1835 edition of Milton's *Poetical Works* (fig.136) have curved bounds.

fig.135 'The Evil Spirit' c.1832

Vignettes are now often interpreted as allowing a mode of representation closer to the experience of vision, because the scene fades out towards the edges, representing peripheral vision: '[At] the perimeter of the vignette ... the sharpness of detail and subsequent fading outwards indicate the spectator's field of vision.'[108] However, vignettes were not always seen as necessarily strictly representational of the visual world.[109] In particular, Ruskin argued that because of the small size of vignettes, viewers experience them differently to paintings. Using a quite different argument to that about the bounds of paintings, he praised Turner's vignettes not because they replicate the circular field of view, but because they do *not* aim to: 'The light and lovely shapelessness of the vignette ... [indicates] to the eye that it is not a picture, but part of one, which it contemplates and, therefore, that it is to choose a much greater distance of position than in the ordinary case – all the small engravings from Turner ... are executed on this principle.'[110] Ruskin insisted Turner's vignettes should be viewed from far away so that 'we feel as if we might see more if we chose, beyond the dreamy and undecided limit.'[111] Thus, we are presented with two quite contradictory interpretations of the optical purpose of Turner's vignettes.

fig.136 Edward Goodall after J.M.W. Turner, 'The Fall of the Rebel Angels' 1835

Turner's vortical works and vignettes often have a strong centralising tendency. As shown earlier, this is true of many of his pictures. His central compositions are sometimes the fruit of perspective (figs.69, 70), and sometimes the product of the disposition of light (figs.84–5). In his

fig.134 'The Angel Standing in the Sun' exh.1846

later work, Turner successfully achieved such central compositions in the most unpromising circumstances: pictures that consist almost entirely of sea and sun can nevertheless have a forcefully dominant centre.[112] As in other works, the powerful focus of Turner's vortices depends on both space and light – they are sometimes so closely related that it is hard to distinguish one from the other.[113] The pictures have been described as 'centrifugal' ('tending to move away from the centre'), but 'centripetal' ('tending towards the centre') may be a better description as it suggests that the light and the perspective serve to unify and pull the picture together, rather than to throw it apart.[114]

Whatever the optical and compositional purposes underlying Turner's vignettes and vortices (and there is no reason to conclude that they aim at only one single effect), they undoubtedly create striking picture spaces. They contain many curves in addition to those of their bounds and are not restricted by rectilinearity. They represent yet further ways of adapting standard perspective to take into account aspects of the experience of vision.

Indifferent or Inspired? Turner's Attitude to Linear Perspective

Turner rarely passed over an opportunity to emphasise stormy seas and swelling waters, or shooting flames and swirling vapours. Even so, his most vague, brief and nebulous pictures almost all have clear fore-, middle- and backgrounds, with identifiable horizons and clear recession into distance. Turner kept firm control of his picture spaces to avoid unintended and disconcerting discontinuities of scale or distance. Some of Turner's individual figures or objects may be barely legible, but it is untrue to say, for example, that he 'destroy[ed] the perspective box' to give an 'informal space to which the concept of a uniform grid or matrix seems alien'.[115]

Distance not only reduces the scale of forms, but also softens their outlines and modifies their colours. This is the concern of aerial perspective, which Turner used extensively, but discussed rarely. He was clear it had nothing to do with geometry: 'Though linear perspective is reducable to rule ... aerial [perspective] cannot come under any geometrical rule and is only to be attained by observation.'[116] Aerial perspective consists 'of parts of light, shade and colour'.[117] In his lectures Turner explained that artists were striving for 'gradation'. Indeed, 'gradation ... is the end, the mead of all our toil in representation; and to this every department of the art is directed, looks and labours to attain, although by different means.'[118] To achieve effective 'gradation', artists need to make use of all elements at their disposal. It may be obtained 'by lines, by light, by shade, by reflexes, by distance: comparatively and relatively'.[119]

Turner's pictures show that pictorial space is created with much more than linear perspective alone. For example, light does not only contribute to aerial perspective, it also helps to define geometrical depth. While Turner's sun may dissolve forms and boundaries, it does not dissolve space, but orders it.[120] Light often defines space more strongly than any other element; it works with linear perspective to create coherent three-dimensional worlds. Colour also plays its part. Many of Turner's compositions originated in 'colour structures' – designs consisting of pure washes of colour – with geometrical recession overlaid later. Sometimes colour and line coincide. Even if not, they often coexist in a balanced tension that does not disrupt geometrical space, but stabilises it.[121]

However, in spite of Turner's claims in his lectures, 'gradation' was not the only aim of his art. He used colour and light to do much more than simply create a superficially accurate representation of the three-dimensional world on a two-dimensional surface. In addition to the layers of literary meaning he encompassed in his works, Turner searched beyond outward appearances in order to hunt out the essence of the natural world.

Linear perspective was one of his weapons. It enabled him to disassemble individual forms, depicting them from many directions, before reconstructing them in an ideal form from a single viewpoint. It enabled him to capture the boundless expanses of landscape and the scale of humankind's architectural achievements. Above all it enabled him to communicate his discoveries.

In a statement quoted at the beginning of this chapter, Sir Walter Armstrong suggested that Turner neglected perspective, and that he did this through either ignorance or indifference. It should now be evident that Armstrong failed to detect a whole area of Turner's artistic achievement. Turner was not ignorant of perspective, and certainly was not indifferent to it. His picture spaces may not have been calculated mathematically, and may be softer and rounder than those produced by a rigorous adherence to standard perspective, but the principles of perspective enter into the foundations of his works and give unity, coherence and balance. Turner was inspired by the tradition of standard perspective and sometimes modified that tradition in a quite inspirational way. But he did not discard standard perspective and all his spatial shifts are carefully and subtly planned variations of it. As early as 1843, Ruskin came to the same conclusion about Turner's use of perspective:

> I will not say he is immaculate, but whenever he errs, he errs, I think, not palpably – *certainly* not in ignorance – but to obtain some particular grace or harmony of line, in places where he thinks the error will not be detected.'[122]

Notes to Chapter 1

1. RA General Assembly Minutes, 10 Dec. 1807. Turner attracted twenty-seven votes for, and one against. The identity of the dissenter is not recorded. Note that in the catalogue of the Turner bicentennial exhibition the date of election is given as 2 November 1807 (*Turner*, exh. cat., Tate Gallery 1974, p.196) and this is repeated in, for example, *J.M.W. Turner*, Grand Palais, Paris 1983, p.311 and Andrew Wilton, *Turner in his Time*, 1987, pp.78 and 85. 2 November was in fact the date on which summonses were issued for the election.

2. Thomas Malton [Senior], *A Compleat Treatise on Perspective in Theory and Practice on the True Principles of Dr Brook Taylor*, 1775 (Malton 1775); later editions 1776, 1778, 1779. In 1783 Thomas Malton Senior published an extensive *Appendix, or Second Part, to the Compleat Treatise...* (Malton 1783). James Malton, *The Young Painter's Maulstick, Being a Practical Treatise on Perspective* 1800 (Malton 1800).

3. Turner became a full Academician on 12 Feb. 1802; he was a member of the RA Council during 1803 and 1804. He had submitted his candidature for professor of perspective by 16 March 1807 (RA Council Minutes).

4. British Library Add MS 46151 C f.3r (abbreviated here to MS C). This is from the first full draft of Turner's lecture 1. There are several other versions of the passage, and they have been drawn on for clarification. As with all quotations from Turner's lectures, this has been edited; in particular, punctuation has been added, and spelling regularised. The Academy certainly needed Turner's help; it had always had difficulties with the professorship of perspective and had not held public lectures on perspective since the late 1770s (in fact, such lectures had been given in only about a quarter of the years of the Academy's existence). The first professor of perspective, Samuel Wale (?1721–86), was appointed in 1768, the year of the RA's foundation. He became ill and gave only private lessons from his house after about 1778 (Hans Hammelmann and T.S.R. Boase, *Book Illustrators in Eighteenth-Century England*, New Haven and London 1975, p.89). Edward Edwards (1738–1806) was appointed in 1788 as teacher of perspective, regularly giving twenty private lessons each winter until his death (Whitley 1913, p.205). He could not be professor because he was only an associate member of the Royal Academy. The architectural draughtsman Joseph Michael Gandy offered himself as a replacement for Edwards (RA Council Minutes, 26 Feb. 1807) but he too was only an associate and, similarly, could not have delivered public lectures.

5. MS K ff.4r–3r. This is the version of lecture 1 that Turner used in 1811. The passage is described as 'an elogium' in MS B f.3v. In preparation for his lectures, Turner carried out a brief analysis of the length of Reynolds's First and Second Discourses in his *Derbyshire* sketchbook, TB CVI 70r.

6. For discussion of this see Kemp 1990, esp. pp.136, 165, 221, 234–5. For a detailed discussion of the situation at the beginning of the nineteenth century see Lisa Fellows Andrus, *Measure and Design in American Painting 1760–1860*, Garland Outstanding Dissertations in the Fine Arts, New York and London 1977 (originally PhD dissertation, Columbia University, 1976), e.g. pp.285–8.

7. Henry Clarke, *Practical Perspective*, 1776, p.69. A similar comment was made by Charles Hayter, *An Introduction to Perspective Drawing and Painting*, 1813, p.42.

8. Some treatises were less strict than others. In one specific case Kirby 1765 recommended that the rules be ignored (see discussion of lecture 2 in chap.2, below). Thomas Bardwell, *The Practice of Painting and Perspective Made Easy*, 1756 and P.H. de Valenciennes, *Elements de perspective pratique*, Paris 1800, are less strict about rules than most. For Valenciennes (like Turner, a landscape painter) see Kemp 1990, p.228.

9. RA Council Minutes, 19 Dec. 1809.

10. London, Royal Academy, *Abstract of the Constitution and Laws of the Royal Academy of Arts in London*, 1815, pp.18–19. This may be only a summary of the duties of the professor of perspective, which are given in a variety of forms. For example the 1768 founding constitution of the RA includes among the duties 'the projection of shadows, reflections and refractions'.

11. MS B f.2r. There is also a more detailed plan for lecture 1 on f.3v (see discussion of lecture 1 in chap.2, below).

12. MS K f.1v. One example of Turner structuring his course with care was his decision to teach simple techniques of parallel perspective before more complex ones of angular perspective. See discussion of lecture 3 in chap. 2, below.

13. For more details of Turner's use of these works see Ziff 1984. For other examples of Turner's more general early reading see Barry Venning, 'Turner's Annotated Books: Opie's *Lectures on Painting* and Shee's *Elements of Art*', *Turner Studies*, [I], vol.2, no.1, Summer 1982, pp.36–46; [II], vol.2, no.2, Winter 1983, pp.40–9; [III], vol.3, no.1, Summer 1983, pp.33–44.

14. Other works published in Britain that Turner used include ones by: Lamy (1710), Taylor (1715 and 1719), Hamilton (1738), Highmore (1763), Priestley (1770), Ferguson (1775) and James Malton (1800). For older works see n.63 to chap.2, below.

15. He also seems to have had access to unpublished material by Thomas Malton Junior and Samuel Wale, as he discusses their perspective techniques extensively.

16. Turner copied a diagram from Guidobaldo del Monte, *Perspectivae Libri Sex*, Pesaro 1600, p.135 (fig.7) into the *Perspective* sketchbook, TB CVIII 43r (fig.8). He discussed the technique it shows at several places, the earliest in MS A f.16r, and over fifteen years later in MS AA f.10r.

17. MS BB f.62 is a single sheet of paper that contains a translation of a passage about Dürer from the French treatise by Salomon De Caus, *La Perspective avec la raison des ombres et mirroirs*, London [*sic*] 1612. Turner's own copy of Jacques Androuet Du Cerceau, *Leçons de perspective positive*, Paris 1576, contains a handwritten translation into English although it is probably pre-nineteenth century and so not commissioned by Turner. He may have occasionally attempted to translate into English himself – for example there are notes in his hand in a mixture of French and English in the *Frittlewell* sketchbook (TB CXII 77v, 78v) partly from Jan Vredeman de Vries, *Perspective...*, The Hague 1604–5, preface and pt.II, pl.18.

18. e.g. see Venning (n.13, above) and John Gage, 'Turner's Annotated Books: Goethe's *Theory of Colours*', *Turner Studies*, vol.4, no.2, Winter 1984, pp.34–52.

19. For example, he apparently did not notice Kirby's highly significant opinions about marginal distortion until many years after he wrote the first drafts. See discussion of lecture 2 in chap.2, below.

20. He may have done this because he attached more importance to ideas that had been validated through later citation. Particular cases include his citations of the ideas of Algarotti (in fact known via Malton 1800 – see n.22 to chap.2, below) and Taylor (often via Malton 1775).

21. In one case where he used Taylor's treatise directly he claimed a passage was a method for depicting irregular objects themselves, whereas it is in fact for depicting any kind of object *on* an irregular surface (MS G f.4v, based on Taylor 1719, pp.59–61.)

22. RA Council Minutes, 17 Oct. 1809.

23. RA Council Minutes, 15 Dec. 1809.

24. RA Council Minutes, 5 Jan. 1810. John Soane was professor of architecture. In 1810 Soane's architecture lectures were to be the first of the season, this means that the perspective lectures were due to begin in mid-February (RA Council Minutes, 15 Dec. 1809). Note that for subsequent years the perspective lectures were scheduled to be the first of the year (RA Council Minutes, 2 July 1810).

25. The postponement could have been because of a controversy aroused by Soane's lectures (this was so fierce that his lectures were postponed for the next year). In the RA Council Minutes of ?10 Feb. 1810 it is

NOTES TO PP.21–27

recorded that Turner 'agreed to postpone' his lectures until the next season, perhaps suggesting that he was asked to do so. On the other hand, the minute records that he 'was admitted at his request', and a passage in the *Greenwich* sketchbook (TB CII 23r) may be a draft of a request to the Council for extra preparatory time. Possibly Turner felt unable to meet the high standard of presentation set by Soane's lectures of 1810.

26 These are the fine copies made by William Rolls. Three of them are dated between 10 and 15 Feb. 1810.

In full drafts of each lecture that were prepared before 1811 are:

Lec. No.	First Draft	First Copy	Fine, Rolls Copy
1	C	–	K
2	D	E	L
3	F	–	M
4	G	I	N
5	P.C.	H	O
6	P.C.	I	P

C, D, etc. = British Library Add MS 46151
c, D, etc
– = manuscript not known
P.C. = manuscript in private collection.

27 RA Council Minutes, 28 Dec. 1810 for the bas relief. The first lecture was announced in the *Morning Chronicle*, Friday 4 Jan. 1811 (Whitley 1913).

28 MS K ff.1v–2r. However, note that this passage also occurs in the first draft which was ready before the postponed 1810 course (MS C ff.2v–3r). In fact, Turner was not necessarily unusually slow in his preparation. Soane was appointed professor of architecture in 1806, but did not first lecture until 1809, and he was in part spurred into action by a letter in the *Examiner* of 8 Jan. 1809 that criticised the Academy because all lecturers had failed to lecture in the previous year. See A.J. Finberg, *The Life of J.M.W. Turner*, 2nd ed., Oxford 1961, p.154 and Jack Lindsay, *Turner: His Life and Work*, St Albans 1973, p.135.

29 Turner delivered a course of six lectures in 1811, 1812, 1814, 1815, 1816, 1818, 1819, 1821, 1824, 1825, 1827 (four lectures only) and 1828. (Source: Royal Academy Account Books; source first used by Whitley 1913.)

30 The 'Backgrounds' lecture was number 6 in 1811, but in lecture 6 in 1812 Turner investigated 'colour and its effects. Mechanical, natural and poetic combinations were also introduced with ingenous illustrations … appropriate citations from Milton, Thomson and other poets afford[ed] examples of beautiful composition and combination as to harmony and splendor; but when dismembered graphically into parts not only contradict by forced contrast, but even in the hands of a skilful artist would appear but as conceits of a luxurious imagination' (review in the *Sun*, 18 Feb. 1812). This, like most of the reviews cited here, has been taken from the Whitley Papers, vol.12, housed in the British Museum Department of Prints and Drawings. Note that 'Backgrounds' was probably given on at least one occasion additional to 1811, as a note later added to it refers to a fire that took place in October 1816 (see Gage 1969, p.249, n.170). For lecture passages on poetry and painting see Wilton 1990 and Jerrold Ziff, 'J.M.W. Turner on Poetry and Painting', *Studies in Romanticism*, vol.3, no.4. 1964, pp.193–215.

31 Diagrams that suggest the existence of further texts include especially the 'shadow diagrams' numbered 60–76, see below. As first copies exist for lectures 2, 4, 5 and 6 (see n.26), it seems reasonable to assume that they were made also for lectures 1 and 3.

32 MS M began as a copy made by William Rolls in Feb. 1810 (it is signed and dated on f.25v), a great many amendments were made to it, including one on the back of a letter dated 1 Jan. 1827 (now separated from MS M and bound as BB f.56).

33 I am grateful to Peter Bower for this information. See his *Turner's Papers*, exh. cat., Tate Gallery 1990, esp. pp.109–12.

34 *Champion*, 28 Jan. 1816, reviewing lecture 3.

35 *Champion*, 14 Jan. 1816, reviewing lecture 1.

36 *Morning Post*, 10 Jan. 1816, reviewing lecture 1.

37 Richard and Samuel Redgrave, *A Century of British Painters*, 1947 ed., p.258.

38 Ruskin, 1903–12. vol.7, p.446. Ruskin's *Elements of Drawing and Perspective* was published in 1857.

39 MS AA.

40 MS J and MS T.

41 MS M, particularly ff.30v–33v.

42 MSS V, W and X.

43 MS BB ff.66–67. For this and for material on colour in the lectures generally see Gage 1969, esp. pp.209–11 and pp.106 *et seq*.

44 Some of the diagrams are referred to by number on MS BB f.12; this fragment is not a full lecture draft. Others, such as a 'prison drawing' (TB CXCV 120 or 128?) are referred to on [f.10r] of 'Lecture upon light, shade and reflexes' (private collection).

45 In Finberg 1909, section CXCV is devoted to 'Perspective Diagrams', but not all the items in this section are lecture diagrams; for example TB CXCV 156 is simply a study for Turner's watercolour of 'The Pantheon, Oxford Street, the Morning after the Fire' (fig.62). Works such as TB CXCV 155, 157 and 160, while being careful perspective constructions, do not relate to any finished lecture diagrams and so may not be directly associated with the lectures at all.

46 For example TB CXCV 158 (fig.57) is a careful pencil construction, and TB CXCV 159 is a tracing from it, probably made with the intention of producing a lecture diagram, but never completed. TB CXCV 162 and TB CXCV 81 were both abandoned before they were finished.

47 Some of this category of diagrams have sources in Kirby's treatise or Euclid's *Elements*. Others concern, for example, anamorphoses.

48 For example, there are a great many sketch diagrams in the first draft of lecture 5 for which no large diagrams survive.

49 Turner is reported to have used 'many of his rarest drawings', by the Redgraves (n.37 above), p.257. There are references to the showing of prints in: reviews of lecture 1 (e.g. *Sun*, 8 Jan. 1811, where reference is made to 'a print of Raphael's "Transfiguration"' as well as Turner's 'geometrical diagram on the subject' (fig.23); in MS M esp. ff.30v–33v; and throughout lecture 6 (e.g. MS P ff.3v, 7v, 8v, 10r). On 28 Dec. 1810 Turner requested that a bas relief be taken into the lecture room 'to serve as an illustration for his first lecture' (RA Council Minutes, 28 Dec. 1810). The evidence that he may have made diagrams during the lectures is an account (however, written over a quarter of a century after Turner ceased lecturing): 'it is to be regretted that copies of his graphic diagrams, as sketched on the lecture boards, were not preserved with his notes.' (T. Miller, *Turner and Girtin's Picturesque Views Sixty Years Since*, 1854, pp.xlii–xliii, cited by Gage 1987, p.143). Copies of Raphael's cartoons by Sir James Thornhill had been in the possession of the Academy since 1800 (Ziff 1963, p.134, n.33). The copies still exist at the RA, but they are rolled, and in need of conservation.

50 See MS M f.33v (where referred to as diagram number 52*), MS BB f.12r (where referred to as diagram 74), MS BB f.18r. The diagram now bears no number at all, but was apparently attached to a mount or backing bearing the number 52* when Finberg wrote his Inventory of the Turner Bequest (Finberg 1909).

51 TB CXCV 94 (fig.28) was originally numbered 16 and intended to accompany lecture 2; however, it was apparently never used in this way (there is no reference to it in the appropriate place in lecture 2 – MS L) and it was used between diagrams 35 and 36 for lecture 3 (on MS M ff.8v–9r the sequence of diagram references runs 35, 16, 36). The diagram was eventually renumbered 47 and used elsewhere.

52 Review of 24 Jan. 1816, source unknown (Whitley Papers, vol.12, p.1560).

53 MS M f.3r, f.10v, f.15r.

54 *British Press*, 5 Jan. 1819, cited by Gage 1987, p.143.

55 *European Magazine*, Jan. 1824. It is not clear exactly how Turner's lecture diagrams were displayed. The phrasing of the references to diagrams in his manuscripts suggests that he was helped by an assistant.

56 Mumbling: see e.g. Gage 1987, p.97; speed: Farington's Diary for 8 Jan. 1811 reports Turner lecturing 'too fast'; on 28 Jan. 1811 Farington was in the chair for Turner's fourth lecture and recorded in his diary that it lasted only thirty-five minutes.

57 Review of 8 Jan. 1816, source unknown (Whitley Papers, vol.12, p.1560).

58 *New Monthly Magazine*, Feb. 1815.

59 In lecture 6 Turner scribbled in the margin

[105]

'I am sorry I have mislaid the print' – MS P f.3v. The apology for the loss of the portfolio is MS BB f.53v. He returned the favour to Fuseli five years later: on 6 Jan. 1819 Fuseli was indisposed and so could not give his introductory painting lecture; Turner stepped in with his second perspective lecture. (Review of 7 Jan. 1819, source unknown – Whitley Papers, vol.12, p.1560.) The saga of the lost portfolio (which may have in fact been lost two weeks running) is set out in Whitley 1913.

60 References to Turner's stammering when speaking in public were made by W.P. Frith cited in Jack Lindsay, *Turner: The Man and his Art*, 1985, p.63. Ruskin, 1903–12, vol.13, p.307 notes the following from James Ballantine, *Life of David Roberts RA*, 1866, p.238: 'Turner's health was once proposed by an Irishman who had attended the lectures on perspective, on which he complimented the artist. "Turner made a short reply in a jocular way, and concluded by saying, rather sarcastically, that he was glad this honourable gentleman had profited so much by his lectures as thoroughly to understand perspective, for it was more than he did."'

61 Brian Butterworth, 'Was Turner Dyslexic?', *Turner Studies*, vol.11, no.1, Summer 1991, pp.5–6. This article sets out to prove that Turner was not dyslexic, countering claims made by Wilton 1990. The article is convincing in its arguments, but it is unfortunate that one of the lecture texts consulted for the purposes of assessing Turner's spelling is not in fact in his handwriting but is a copy by an unknown hand (MS I). Also, this lecture, and MS P, as transcribed by Ziff 1963, is normally described as lecture 6, not 4, see n.26, above. These errors do not necessarily invalidate Butterworth's conclusions, but they do mean that some of the detailed results are irrelevant to anything but an assesment of the writing abilities of the unidentified copyist who wrote the main text in MS I.

62 MS M f.33r, f.10r, f.33v. Slip of paper f.17 was originally affixed to f.18r. To add to Turner's self-inflicted difficulties, 'the Ionic' actually is on p.29 and not p.19!

63 *Sun*, 22 Jan. 1811.

64 Letter from Turner to John Taylor, reviewer in the *Sun* – see John Gage (ed.), *Collected Correspondence of J.M.W. Turner*, Oxford 1980, letter number 38.

65 For Reynolds's performance, see Gage 1987, p.93. For Fuseli, whose lectures were 'spoken of as being pedantic' while Turner's were 'much laughed at as being ignorant and ill-written', see Farington's Diary for 10 Feb. 1812.

66 For details of the parliamentary inquiry see Gage 1987, pp.144–5, Whitley 1913, p.259 and William Sandby, *The History of the Royal Academy*, 1868, vol.2, pp.81–2.

67 Copy of a letter by Fry, now bound as British Library Add MS 46151 BB ff.74r-v.

68 Particularly Jerrold Ziff, John Gage, Eric Shanes (see Select Bibliography); Barry Venning (see n.13 above); and Jack Lindsay (see nn.28 and 60 above).

Notes to Chapter 2

1 *Sun*, 8 Jan. 1811.
2 MS B f.3v.
3 MS K f.6v. Turner is probably referring to the 'Windsor Leoni' volume of Leonardo drawings and manuscripts that is still in the British Royal Collection, which it entered in the seventeenth century (*Leonardo da Vinci*, exh. cat., Hayward Gallery 1989, p.18).
4 MS K f.7r, based on Giovanni Paolo Lomazzo, *A Tracte Containing the Artes of Curious Paintinge, Carvinge and Buildinge*, trans. by R. Haydocke, Oxford 1598, p.17. Michelangelo's rule was in fact that figures should be 'multiplied by one, two and three' (see Ziff 1984, p.49, n.7). Turner was not the only one to fail to understand this strange requirement. According to Benjamin Ralph, *The School of Raphael, or the Students' Guide to Expression in History Painting*, 1759, p.5: 'Michelangelo ... according to Lomazzo [told his pupil Marcus de Seneca] "that he should make a figure pyramidal, serpentlike, and multiplied by one, two and three" which precept, as the author of the Analysis [i.e. William Hogarth?] observes, hath remained a mystery down to this time; and indeed it appears not only mysterious but absurd.'
5 This diagram is number 10, and was used in this capacity later in the lecture. However, it is also referred to on MS K f.7r, and a contemporary review notes its use in this context in the lecture (*Examiner*, 13 Jan. 1811, given by Whitley 1913, p.206).
6 MS K f.7r. The diagrams are based on ones in Albrecht Dürer's *Proportions of the Human Body* (1st ed., 1528).
7 For Turner's use of Junius here see Ziff 1984, esp. p.47.
8 His observations are recorded in the *Windmill and Lock* sketchbook, TB CXIV 12v–13r (fig.19), 17r, 19v, 20r, 31r, 34r.
9 Turner made notes about viewing the church, also in the *Windmill and Lock* sketchbook, TB CXIV 64r, 67r, 76v.
10 MS K ff.13r–v. The use of perspective drawings by architects in the early nineteenth century is briefly discussed in Gavin Stamp, *The Great Perspectivists*, 1982.
11 Turner was thinking particularly about the illustrations in James Stuart and Nicholas Revett, *The Antiquities of Athens*, vol.1, 1762, from which he made notes and, for a later version of the lecture, copied diagrams (e.g. TB CXCV 169, 170 and 171, which are discussed in MS J and based on notes in MS BB ff.33–4, taken from Stuart and Revett, pp.42–7 and pls. II and VI).
12 MS K f.13v.
13 MS K ff.14v–15r.
14 MS K ff.16r–v. I have also drawn on MS J ff.14r–15v for my discussion of figs.21 and 22. (Turner's comment about domes insignificant above their porticoes evokes the National Gallery! However, it was not designed until the 1830s, by William Wilkins.)
15 MS K f.15v. The point is part of a theoretical (but not practical) objection Turner had about depicting buildings parallel to the picture plane. In the MS J version of the material (see n.14), Turner introduced yet another problematic diagram (TB CXCV 172). The difficulty with that, he explained, is that it is in perspective, but completely unshaded.
16 MS K f.16v.
17 MS K f.4v.
18 MS K f.5r.
19 MS K f.5v.
20 For his account of Renaissance perspective, Turner's main source was Matthew Pilkington, *Dictionary of Painters*, 1770. He seems to have skimmed through the entries for individual artists until a mention of perspective caught his eye (see notes in the *Perspective* sketchbook, TB CVIII 5v–6r, 27v). He had little choice, as no history of the use of perspective by artists had yet been written in English.
21 MS K f.6r.
22 MS K ff.6r–v. The passage is actually quoted from Malton 1800, p.ii (via Turner's original notes MS BB f.3r), not directly from Francesco Algarotti, *An Essay on Painting*, 1764.

[106]

23 This attitude is also evident in Turner's rivalry with the young painter David Wilkie, whose rapid rise to fame he criticised in the period 1806–10, just at the same time he was working on the lecture drafts. See Arthur S. Marks, 'Rivalry at the Royal Academy: Turner, Wilkie and Bird', *Studies in Romanticism*, vol.20, 1981, pp.333–62.
24 MS K ff.18v–19r.
25 The analysis is contrived because the lines illustrating the geometry of the 'Transfiguration' could be positioned almost anywhere (as Turner's pencil underdrawing shows). Turner performed further (equally contrived and varied) analyses of the picture's geometry in MS C f.15r and MS A f.4r.
26 MS K f.21r, referring particularly to Reynolds's First Discourse, line 104 (ed. Robert R. Wark, New Haven and London 1975).
27 MS L ff.1r–v. The passage was adapted from one in Malton 1775, pp.5–6. In Malton this material was part of a discussion of optics, but Turner changed its emphasis to make it into a statement of the purpose of perspective.
28 See p.84.
29 MS L f.1v.
30 MS L f.1v.
31 MS L f.1v, based on footnote to Malton 1775, p.13.
32 MS L f.2r, both passages paraphrased from Malton 1775, p.18. The diagram (fig.25) is based on one that Turner copied into the *Perspective* sketchbook from Lomazzo (TB CVIII 60v, from Lomazzo (see n.4) bk. v, p.204). Although the diagram includes both the names 'Lamatius' (i.e. Lomazzo) and Moxon, there is no similar diagram in Joseph Moxon, *Practical Perspective*, 1670. In fact, Moxon does not even use the terminology referred to in the diagram.
33 MS L f.2v. Diagram in TB CVIII f.3v (fig.5) is taken from Salomon De Caus, *La perspective avec la raison des ombres et mirroirs*, London [sic] 1612, tenth theorem (pages unnumbered, f.6r). See chap.1 above for more discussion of this standard model of perspective.
34 See, for example, MS M f.3r.
35 Malton 1775, pp.42–3.
36 MS D f.2r. Turner seems a little unsure, as in the first copy he commented, 'according to some opinions, *perhaps doubtful however*, he has left much tautology' (MS E f.3v, my emphasis).
37 Malton 1775, p.55 'Taylor's second treatise' is the 1719 edition of *Linear Perspective*, which is very different to the 1715 edition.
38 MS D f.4r.
39 MS L f.6v based on Malton 1775, p.89.
40 In the twentieth century 'curvilinear perspective' is normally used to mean a perspective system in which lines that are straight in real life are represented by ones that are curved on the picture surface. However, Turner used the term to refer to the use of standard perspective to depict curved objects.
41 Charles Alphonse Du Fresnoy, *The Art of Painting*, trans. W. Mason with annotations by Joshua Reynolds, York 1783, pp.14–15 (lines 162–9).
42 MS L ff.7r–v.
43 MS L f.7v. Notes by Reynolds in Du Fresnoy (see n.41), p.83.
44 MS L f.9r.
45 Fig.29 is based on figures in Malton 1775. Fig.30 is based on one copied from John Hamilton, *Stereography*, 1738, fig.84 no.1 into the *Perspective* sketchbook, TB CVIII 18r. 'Emmerson' is William Emerson, *The Elements of Optics in Four Books*, 1768, who Malton does mention along with Hamilton at this point. There is no evidence that Turner consulted Emerson directly.
46 The diagram is based on a sketch in MS L f.10v, which is itself loosely based on Malton 1775, pl.VII, figs.33–4. Both of Malton's diagrams have a different emphasis from Turner's. The idea of apparent diameters was fairly commonly discussed in British eighteenth-century perspective treatises.
47 MS N ff.3r–2v.
48 MS D f.7r, following Lamy 1710 pp.35–6. Turner often referred to Lamy as 'the Jesuit'; this was a confusing thing to do as the name was usually given to Jean Dubrueil, a different French author on perspective whose treatise was also translated into English.
49 The diagrams could be partly based on Lamy 1710, pls.20 and 21.
50 MS D f.7r, based on Lamy 1710, p.119.
51 In the early drafts of lecture 2, Turner seems to suggest that Kirby and Malton had similar views. He simply did not notice what Kirby said. Eventually, but almost certainly after 1811, he did make notes on Kirby's controversial comments – MS F f.20r.
52 Malton 1775, p.101.
53 See p.77 and fig.99.
54 MS L f.15r. Turner was thinking particularly of Rubens's ceiling painting that was at Osterly House.
55 MS L f.16v. Some of these further objections are discussed, along with fig.94, in chap.3, below.
56 MS M f.32r (this originally followed directly from MS L f.16v but is now differently arranged).
57 MS L f.17r. This is a variant ending to lecture 2 that replaced that now at MS M f.32r (see n.56).
58 MS M ff.1r–v. The plan for the lectures is given on pp.18–19 above.
59 MS M f.1v. Turner felt that parallel perspective could not 'bear the tests of nature'; his recommendations about the use of parallel perspective in paintings are examined in chap.3, below.
60 In part this was because he was not aware that objects at forty-five degrees to the picture plane can be depicted with techniques of parallel perspective and do not require ones of angular perspective. Also see n.65.
61 A few eighteenth- and early nineteenth-century perspective treatises, such as Kirby (see n.62) and Malton 1783, include a selection of historical methods of perspective, but none of them cover as many as Turner was to examine, although they do tend to go into more detail about each individual method than Turner. The first full history of perspective was Noel G. Poudra, *Histoire de la perspective ancienne et moderne*, Paris 1864, which is far more extensive than Turner's study.
62 Kirby 1765 includes methods that he attributes to Marolois, Vignola, Vredeman de Vries, Pozzo, and Dubreuil.
63 In the 1811 course Turner discussed in detail or mentioned methods that he attributed to: '1505' (i.e. Viator/Jean Pelerin); Androuet du Cerceau (treatise first published, and edition Turner used, 1576); 'Ubaldus, 1600' (Guidobaldo del Monte); *Marolois, 1614 (treatise first published 1614); *Vignola, 1644 (treatise first published 1583); *Vredeman 'Friese', 1619 (Vredeman de Vries, treatise first published 1604–5); Accolti, 1625; Sirigatti, 1625 (treatise first published 1596); Niceron 1643 (treatise first published 1646 – Turner made an error); Moxon, 1670; *Pozzo, 1700. As part of his research he had also studied methods by: De Caus, 1612; Scheiner, 1653; Troili, 1683; Barbaro, 1568; Aleaume and Mignon, 1643; Lautensack, 1564 and two unidentified methods, one dated 1577. He consulted original treatises, except for those marked with an asterisk which he knew from Kirby.
64 MS M f.8r.
65 Turner simply placed both the vanishing points at the same distance from the eye, whereas they should be located by drawing lines parallel to the sides of the plan of the house from the eye/distance point at the top until they intersect the horizon. These intersections are the vanishing points. Unless the building was at forty-five degrees to the picture plane (represented by the base line in his construction), these vanishing points would be at different distances from the centre. In the diagram of the house (fig.40) the plan is definitely not at forty-five degrees.
66 In MS M, a lecture certainly ended on f.16v in one season, and possibly on f.22r in another. The only known reviews of lectures 3 and 4 for 1811 are brief, but are consistent with them both consisting of material in MS M (i.e. material that was originally in the early drafts of lecture 3 alone). There is a great amount of extra material in MS M, the lecture text of lecture 3 and, it is proposed here, lecture 4. Some of this extra material, particularly ff.30v–33v, was definitely used in a lecture in at least one season (although not necessarily 1811), and there are several diagrams that accompany it. including figs.28 and 14. The fine copy of lecture 4 (MS N, made in Feb. 1810 by

William Rolls) was not at all heavily revised – some sides such as ff.4r, 4v, 9r, 9v, 10r, 12r, 12v contain no amendments at all – and contains no references to large lecture diagrams, even though there are a number of sketch diagrams in the first draft (MS G).

67 *Perspective* sketchbook, TB CVIII 46r, based on Lorenzo Sirigatti, *La pratica della prospettiva*, Venice 1625, cap.32.

68 Staircases, Sirigatti (n.67), lib.I, caps.20–5, and fiddles, cap.31.

69 MS F f.9v.

70 MS M f.13r. In spite of his disapproval Turner never criticised Sirigatti's approach as strongly as Kirby, who published an entire book attacking it: *Dr Brook Taylor's Method of Perspective, Compared with Examples lately Published on this Subject as Sirigatti's by Isaac Ware* [?1757].

71 MS M f.19v.

72 MS M f.20v.

73 This problem, and Turner's views about it, are discussed in chap.3, below.

74 MS M f.24v.

75 MS G f.9v (the first draft of lecture 4, drawing also on the first copy, MS I ff.34v–35r).

76 I have not studied lecture 5 in as much depth as I have lectures 2, 3 and 4 and it remains to be studied in detail. I hope that the outline presented here may inspire others to make the attempt!

77 MS O f.1r.

78 MS O ff.1r–2r.

79 Note, however, that this is just an impression. The lecture remains to be set in its early nineteenth-century context. See n.76.

80 MS O f.2v. Turner took this idea from a footnote to Malton 1775, pp.29–30. Malton in fact calls the gap 'the space of its activity' and rejects the idea. See also pp.83–4 above and MS H f.11v.

81 MS O f.3v.

82 MS H f.4v. (earlier version of MS O).

83 MS O f.4r.

84 MS O f.4v.

85 First draft of lecture 5 (private collection), [f.3r] (sides not numbered). Elements of this discussion may have their origins in notes in the *Perspective* sketchbook that seem to be built up from Gerard de Lairesse, *The Art of Painting*, English trans., 1738 (TB CVIII 82v–91v). See Gage 1969, esp. p.178

86 MS O f.5r. The 'Rembrandt' referred to is in the Fitzwilliam Museum, Cambridge. It is currently attributed to Rembrandt's workshop.

87 MS H ff.6r–v.

88 MS H ff.7r–7v. I have been unable to identify the source of the passage that Turner quotes.

89 Identification of 'The Fall of the Clyde' (Walker Art Gallery, Liverpool) made by Gage 1969, p.41.

90 MS O f.7r.

91 Ibid.

92 MS H f.8v.

93 MS H f.8v, 9r.

94 MS O ff.8v–9r.

95 John Gage has published Turner's discussion of the same portrait from the *Greenwich* sketchbook (TB CII 15r–16r), and identified it with Van Dyck's 'Portrait of Lady Southampton' in Melbourne (Gage 1969, p.198).

96 MS H ff.12r–v.

97 MS H ff.13v–14r. There is a slightly different version in MS O, with, for example, 'practice' substituted for 'the mind' and 'endless' for 'useless'. The Reynolds passage referred to is from the Twelfth Discourse, lines 59–63 (ed. Wark, see n.26), where the context is different: 'the minds of men [*sic*] are so very differently constituted, that it is impossible to find one method which shall be suitable to all. It is of no use to prescribe to those who have no talents; and those who have talents will find methods for themselves, methods dictated to them by their own particular dispositions, and by the experience of their own particular necessities.'

98 *Sun*, 5 Feb. 1811. It is not possible to determine which material may have augmented the fine copy of lecture 5 in MS O.

99 *Sun*, 15 Feb. 1811.

100 MS B f.2r.

101 Published in full by Ziff 1963.

102 Turner seems uncertain about the horizon height: elsewhere he discusses how the low horizon elevates the figure – see p.69.

103 MS P f.3r.

104 The paper of TB CXCV 168 (fig.55) is watermarked 1812. The diagram is unnumbered and its association with this part of the lectures is speculative.

105 Titian: MS P ff.10r–v. Poussin: MS P ff.14v. See also p.69.

106 Some passages are added to the first draft of lecture 6 (private collection), e.g. [f.5v, f.7r] (sides not numbered). Other parts are added to the fine copy, e.g. MS P ff.3r, 10v.

107 MS P ff.19v–20r.

Notes to Chapter 3

1 Sir Walter Armstrong, *Turner*, 1902, p.83.

2 W.L. Wyllie, *J.M.W. Turner*, 1905, p.45.

3 These preparatory studies include TB CXCV 82, TB CXCV 91, TB CXCV 98 (fig.58), TB CXCV 111 (fig.59), and TB CXCV 158 (fig.57). Note that the vanishing points in these diagrams may not always be correct as Turner seems to have been unsure about their position – see n.65 to chap.2, above. Also included in the 'Perspective Diagrams' section of the Turner Bequest are three careful perspective constructions of classical buildings, but these are unfinished and do not correspond to any large lecture diagrams (TB CXCV 155, 157 and 160). There are no other drawings in the Turner Bequest in which an attempt has been made to carry out a full perspective construction.

4 Turner seems to have carried out a quite lengthy procedure to locate the measure point, but unnecessarily, as it could have been positioned simply by drawing a single arc centred on the vanishing point, from the eye/distance point to the horizon. The diagram contains much further construction that seems superfluous.

5 The shadows do not seem to have been geometrically constructed, but determined by eye.

6 Fig.48 is in watercolour over ruled pencil, but no new construction was carried out to determine the position of the ruled lines, which seem to have been copied from fig.59. Fig.49 is based on a tracing from fig.48. There are several differences between figs.48 and 49 and the preparatory study (fig.59), particularly that the verticals slope in the finished diagrams – see p.74 below.

7 For example, the finished lecture diagrams TB CXCV 79 and 80 (figs.39 and 40) demonstrate a plan-based method, but Turner did not use a plan to prepare TB CXCV 83, on which they are based.

8 For Malton see p.15, above; for Hardwick see *Turner and Architecture*, exh. cat., Tate Gallery 1988, p.8; Gage 1969, pp.22–3; Gage 1987, p.23, esp. n.7; and A.J. Finberg, *Notes on Three of Turner's Architectural Drawings*, 1920.

9 In fig.61 the vanishing points are not even at the same height. The drawing is probably based directly on a freehand sketch in the *Oxford* sketchbook (TB II 9r), that was squared for transfer. Turner sometimes noted measurements of parts of buildings when he sketched them, but there

is no evidence that he ever put these to use in a perspective construction. Other works of this period in which Turner made use of vanishing points and ruled lines are also inaccurate. For example 'Christ Church Oxford' of 1790–1 (TB VIII A), in which lines were ruled to vanishing points, but there is no consistent horizon line on which the vanishing points of horizontal lines all fall.

10 Turner corrected the angle of the line of the floor to the right of the lectern. There is an inaccurately drawn line high on the right-hand wall, and the table at the left-hand side does not share a vanishing point with the building (suggesting it may not be exactly parallel to the wall), although the bench alongside it does. For the role of the perspective centre point as a vanishing point, see p.64 below.

11 See Patrick Youngblood, 'The Stones of Oxford: Turner's Depiction of Oxonian Architecture', *Turner Studies*, vol.3, no.2, Winter 1984, p.17, but note that Youngblood exaggerates the difference between the drawing and the watercolour by saying, erroneously, that the drawing is a 'vertical view'.

12 Inaccuracies of note include: high parts of the right-hand wall slope too steeply, and those at the left-hand side not steeply enough, compared to lines lower down. The identification of this view (TB L F) as New College Chapel has been made in the revision of the first part of Finberg's inventory (copy in the Clore Gallery Study Room). It was previously thought to be the chapel at All Souls. Other works which are based on a similar ruled framework include TB L D; TB L E; TB XXXVI F; and TB XLIV V. TB L E does not have consistent vanishing points.

13 Wilton 1980, no.15 says the drawing was 'made on the spot during a tour of 1794', and *Turner and Architecture*, exh. cat., Tate Gallery 1988, no.7 says it was 'made on a visit to Ely'. See also n.63 below.

14 For examples of finished watercolours that were based on several sketches see Finley 1980. He discusses Turner's approach on pp.91–3 and 156–7. He also gives many further examples, e.g. pp.104–5, 109–13, 121–2, 151, 216–17. Note that Finley seems to suggest that Turner was not fully competent at 'produc[ing] a composite image from the various viewpoints' until the early 1830s (p.157), but Turner could in fact do this much earlier. As just one early instance of Turner studying a building from several viewpoints, with great benefit to his finished watercolours of it, see Youngblood 1984 (n.11 above), p.11. For an example of the deliberate omission of details of a building when sketching see *Turner and Architecture*, 1988, no.14. Also see Powell 1991.

15 Ruskin 1903–12, vol.7, p.243. Wilton has noted that when Turner studied from nature he sometimes seems to have considered the appearance that a finished work would take and adjusted his sketch accordingly: 'It is characteristic of him that he should ... have superimposed a conception of a finished work of art onto his initial vision of the landscape' (Wilton 1986, p.408). As Turner manipulated space in similar ways in both his studio works and on-the-spot sketches, distinctions do not normally have to made between them when investigating many aspects of their perspective. Turner's alteration of topography is particularly clear when he produced works based on ones by other artists. See, for an example of this, his 'View near Jubberah', based on a drawing by the amateur artist George Francis White (*Turner: The Fifth Decade*, exh. cat., Tate Gallery 1992, nos.55–6).

16 Ruskin 1903–12, vol.7, pp.44–5.

17 For Turner's idealism see Shanes 1990, e.g. pp.241 *et seq.* and pp.291 *et seq.*

18 Ruskin 1903–12, vol.12, pp.356–7.

19 W 333; see Gage 1987, p.23. For further examples of Turner's work for architects in the 1790s see Susan Morris, '"Two Perspective Views": Turner and Lewis William Wyatt', *Turner Studies*, vol.2, no.2, Winter 1983, pp.34–6.

20 MS C f.2v.

21 Turner was in a similar position to Reynolds, who also had to teach a set of principles that he did not unswervingly follow. See Wilton 1980, p.66.

22 For example, work on Piero della Francesca (see the classic article by R. Wittkower and B.A.R. Carter, 'The Perspective of Piero della Francesca's "Flagellation"', *Journal of the Warburg and Courtauld Institutes*, vol.16, 1953, pp.292–302; but see also Kemp 1990, pp.30–2 for later literature); Vermeer (see Kemp 1990, pp.194–6); and Caillebotte (see K. Vardenoe, *Gustave Caillebotte*, New Haven and London, 1987, especially essay written with Peter Galassi).

23 MS T f.5r. It is important to recognise the difference between the surface geometry of a picture and its perspective. Although Turner occasionally blurred his terminology and so confused the two, for example in his discussion of Raphael's 'Transfiguration' in lecture 1 (see p.36), his understanding of perspective went much further than regarding it as an aid to pattern-making and it is not true that he 'equated perspective with linear pictorial structure', as one author has recently suggested (Shanes 1990, p.202). The visual effects created in a picture depend mainly on 'the visual concentration and direction ... [given] by the coordinates of the flat and frontal picture' (Puttfarken 1986, p.161). This compositional geometry can be enhanced by its relationship to the perspective scheme, but is separate from it. For further discussion of the problems that arise when perspective and composition are treated as coincident see Hagen 1986, pp.125–6.

24 *Champion*, 21 Jan. 1816, review of lecture 2. The material in question is probably a version of that given at the beginning of lecture 3 in 1811.

25 There are numerous compositional studies in which Turner establishes a spatial scheme by means of lines receding to vanishing points. For example, a study for 'Aeneas and the Sibyl' (TB LI N); pages in the *Studies for Pictures: Isleworth* sketchbook (TB XC including 11v, 58v); and TB LXX R, in which the direction of the brushstrokes further reinforces the perspective scheme. For a discussion of a sheet in which Turner concerns himself with 'alternative systems of organising recession and the interconnectedness of planes' see the discussion of TB CXX B in Wilton 1986, p.411. Brief sketches from nature which emphasise linear aspects of the perspective include several compositions in the *Grenoble* sketchbook (TB LXXIV, e.g. 69, 86, 90v, 91).

26 That is, the perspective centre is that point on the picture surface from which a perpendicular line will meet the artist's eye. Throughout, it is assumed that all the perpendicular lines under discussion are horizontal.

27 In this case the perspective scheme coincides exactly with the compositional scheme. See n.23 and see Puttfarken 1986 for more discussion of the importance of this coincidence in central compositions.

28 MS M f.2r.

29 Edwards 1803, pp.285–6. For Edwards at the Royal Academy see n.4 to chap.1.

30 MS M f.31r. Turner's reason for finding this effect reprehensible (he particularly cites the work of Giulio Romano as an instance) is perhaps because a viewpoint (i.e. perspective centre) outside the picture would lessen the possibility of unity of effect (see below).

31 Nicholson 1990, p.249 discusses this 'unexpected gulf that the eye must bridge' and also relates the space to Claude's 'Landscape with Jacob, Laban and Daughters' (Petworth), to which 'Palestrina – Composition' was painted as a companion. Claude is, of course, an artist who made great use of central perspective structures.

32 Both Wilton and Paulson discuss the different speeds of Turner's recessions (e.g. Wilton 1986, p.419, Paulson 1982, p.71). Paulson goes further: 'One channel, usually off to the left or right side of the picture is man-made ... The other, which is usually more central, is a natural force almost always emanating from the sun.' (p.72)

33 For example, Turner did not generally place significant action at the centre of his pictures, nor did he restrict his pictures to what could be seen at a single glance of the eye (see below). Furthermore, the relationship between the perspective centre and the physical centre is extremely varied in Turner's work. For perspective and unity of effect, unity of point of view, and unity of action see, for example, Thomas Puttfarken, 'David's *Brutus* and Theories of Pictorial

Unity in France', *Art History*, vol.4, no.3, Sept. 1981, pp.291–304; Puttfarken 1986; Michael Fried, *Absorption and Theatricality: Painting and Beholder in the Age of Diderot*, Berkeley, Los Angeles and London 1980, e.g. pp.82–92, 134–5, 156–9; and John Sweetman in *The Panoramic Image*, exh. cat., John Hansard Gallery, Southampton 1981. For wilful avoidance of traditional modes of unity see also Ronald Paulson, *Emblem and Expression: Meaning in English Art of the Eighteenth Century*, London and Cambridge, Mass. 1975, p.229 and Svetlana Alpers, *The Art of Describing: Dutch Art in the Seventeenth Century*, 1989, pbk ed., e.g. p.85.

34 MS M f.2r. Note that although Turner had theoretical objections to the validity of parallel perspective (see discussion of lecture 3 in chap.2, above), he had no hesitation about recommending it, nor about using it.

35 For example, Edward Edwards instructed that when depicting architecture in history paintings, 'leading or principal parts should be disposed parallel to the picture, scarcely ever obliquely or inclined to it ... for all oblique or inclined arrangements of buildings in the background ... produce an unpleasing effect, and destroy the simplicity and grandeur of the picture.' (Edwards 1803, p.289). Another early nineteenth-century author noted: 'We have authorities of no less weight than Canaletti, Gaspar and N. Poussin, Claude Lorraine &c for [the benefits of] viewing the building with one side parallel to the picture, whether the vanishing point of the lines perpendicular to the picture falls in the centre of the horizontal line or not.' (John George Wood, *Six Lectures on the Principles and Practice of Perspective*, 1809, p.8).

36 MS H f.22r.
37 MS C f.17r.
38 MS M f.14v.
39 MS N f.14v. For Turner and Rubens see, for example, Gage 1969, esp. p.64; and Shanes 1990, p.149. For Turner and Poussin see Jerrold Ziff, 'Turner and Poussin', *Burlington Magazine*, vol.105, 1963, pp.315–21; Shanes 1990, esp. p.96 and pp.149–50; and Wilton 1986, although note that Wilton tends to attribute parallel perspective (and central compositions) in Turner's work rather too directly to 'the example of Poussin' (p.423).
40 Works with angular architecture from the late 1830s include: 'Modern Italy – The Pifferari' (RA 1838, B&J 374); 'Ancient Italy – Ovid Banished from Rome' (RA 1838, B&J 375); 'Ancient Rome' (RA 1839, B&J 378) and 'Modern Rome – Campo Vaccino' (RA 1839, B&J 379). In other works from the 1830s such as 'Phryne Going to the Public Baths' (RA 1838, B&J 373) and 'Caligula's Palace and Bridge' (RA 1831, B&J 337) the architecture is varied and not dominated by frontal buildings.
41 MS A ff.14v–15r.
42 MS A f.14v. See also pp.54–5.
43 MS M f.8r.
44 Thomas Malton Senior called for more use of angular perspective when depicting buildings and said that the fact that Canaletto usually depicted architecture parallel to the picture plane was 'a proof, with me, that he was not competent in perspective' (Malton 1783, p.61).
45 MS M f.25r.
46 MS M ff.22r–22v.
47 See discussion of lecture 2 in chap.2, above.
48 MS M f.24r. For the purposes of this discussion it is assumed that the base line is parallel to the bottom of the picture and that the picture plane is vertical.
49 MS M f.25r.
50 MS F f.16r (early version of MS M).
51 MS M f.25v.
52 MS F f.17r. See Thomas Malton Junior, *A Picturesque Tour through the Cities of London and Westminster*, 1792–1801, pls. VI, VII and XII.
53 MS M f.24v.
54 In the late 1830s there was extensive theoretical debate about the representation of vertical convergence. See Martin Kemp, '"Perspective Rectified": Some Alternative Systems in the 19th Century', *AA Files* (London, Architectural Association), vol.15, 1987, pp.30–4. Kemp notes that some pre-nineteenth-century theorists had discussed the problem, but 'it was only in the nineteenth century that sustained attempts were made to establish new systems of perspective' (p.31); these new systems postdate Turner's work for his lectures. See also Kemp 1990, pp.243 *et seq*.
55 The Pulteney Bridge diagrams are based on a careful perspective construction (fig.59). However, the verticals do not slope in this, suggesting that their appearance is something of an afterthought, and they were not constructed according to a fully developed geometrical theory.
56 Butlin and Joll (entry for 'The Decline of Carthage' no.135) quote a review from the *Repository of Arts* for June 1817: 'It is impossible to pass over the execution of the architectural parts of this picture: they are drawn with purity and correctness ... the arrangement of the buildings in perspective is formed with so much adherence to geometrical rule, that the eye is carried through the immense range of magnificent edifices with such rapidity, that we entirely forget the artist and merely dwell upon the historic vision.'
57 Turner did not rule all the lines of the frontal wall, so some are not completely straight.
58 MS L f.15v.
59 Ibid. Turner is probably arguing that from a close point the cornice not only 'dips', but curves downwards.
60 Many earlier artists had noticed standard perspective's failure to incorporate lateral convergence. For example, Leonardo wrote about it (see Kemp 1990, p.49). Lateral convergence itself was discussed *c*.300 BC in the tenth proposition of Euclid's *Optics*. G. Ten Doesschate, *Perspective: Fundamentals, Controversials, History*, Nieuwkoop 1964, p.47 gives it in Latin translation: '...ed manifestum est, quod in elevato iacentia concava apparebunt.'
61 The viewpoint is roughly in line with the dark strip of floor to the left of the inset painting, level with the distant horizon. An appropriate distance is perhaps two to three feet from the picture surface (also see n.64). Nicholson observes that the Claudian landscape, inset in the floor and turned sideways, together with another painting at the foot of the staircase 'literally and figuratively force us to shift our perspective in order to come to terms with what we see' (Nicholson 1990, p.197).
62 Holcomb has noted these effects in Turner's vignettes, especially with animals that seem to 'intrude on the viewer's space' (Holcomb 1970, pp.17–18). While commenting that these devices make the viewer closer to the picture space, Holcomb sees it as part of a 'departure from unified perspective' in Turner's 'Smailholm Tower', an illustration to vol.1 of Sir Walter Scott's *Poetical Works*, but I feel that to relate the spaces of the viewer and the picture does not necessitate the rejection of a consistent three-dimensional picture space. Turner's vignettes are considered below.
63 The scene depicted in 'Ely' is still not quite as large as the field of vision of a single eye at a fixed viewpoint. The vertical angle of view in 'Ely' is perhaps about 100 degrees, whereas that of the human eye is roughly '150 degrees ... rather different from the renaissance window of view' (Hagen 1986, p.12). Nevertheless, 'Ely' encompasses a much wider view than artists usually used, and wider still than theorists recommended. The width of Ely's angle of view 'horizontally' is something over ninety degrees, whereas to avoid risks of distortion (see discussion of lecture 2 in chap.2, above) a more conventional picture may have one of about thirty to sixty degrees. Thomas Malton Senior recommended that the width of the field of view be kept to well under sixty degrees (Malton 1775, p.113). In the 1830s Ruskin argued that objects more than thirty degrees from the central axis of the eye were actually invisible, this meant that the angle of view had to be less than sixty degrees for naturalistic reasons, regardless of any distortion risks: 'No picture may subtend a greater angle than sixty degrees, either in breadth or height' (Ruskin 1903–12, vol.1, p.216 and see pp.98–9, below). Ruskin was wrong: the angle of view of the human visual field with *two* eyes 'extends about one hundred and eighty degrees to the side', according to Hagen (ibid.). See also n.99. It should be noted that 'Ely' does not in fact represent the view from a single viewpoint. so it is not appropriate, or even possible, to specify precise angles and distances of view.
64 I am not, of course, suggesting that Turner actually saw the scene he depicted in 'Hero and Leander'; but, as standard perspective aims to represent a view through a window,

the perspective geometry of an imaginary, studio picture need be no different to that of an on-the-spot sketch. As with 'Ely' (n.63) and almost all of Turner's works, it is not appropriate to attempt to specify an *exact* viewing position for 'Hero and Leander' as its perspective is not geometrically rigorous.

65   Ruskin discussed another aspect of Turner's foregrounds. He argued that 'landscape painters of the old school' all finished their foregrounds too 'clearly and sharply' and so the foregrounds competed with the middle and far distances. But Turner 'introduced a new era in landscape art' and was the first to show that 'it was possible to express immediate proximity to the spectator, without giving anything like completeness to the forms of the near objects ... by a decisive imperfection, a firm, but partial assertion of form, which the eye feels indeed to be close home to it, and yet cannot rest upon, nor cling to, nor entirely understand, and from which it is driven away by necessity to those parts of distance on which it is intended to repose' (Ruskin 1903–12, vol.3, pp.322–3). Ruskin was primarily concerned with the idea that the eye cannot simultaneously focus on near and far objects. The influence of this on Turner's foregrounds is rather tenuous (as Ruskin himself later admitted – see ibid., p.319). A similar comment was made by Sir George Beaumont, who saw the same effect, but deplored it: 'Turner finishes his distances and middle distances upon a scale that requires *universal precision* throughout his pictures – but his foregrounds are comparative *blots*, & faces of figures without a feature being expressed.' (Joseph Farington's Diary, 3 May 1803, quoted in Shanes 1990, p.299).

66   Andrew Wilton, *Turner Abroad,* 1982, p.75 dates this work to 1845 and places it as one of Turner's last European views.

67   This is a subject too vast to examine here. For some its implications see Michael Fried, *Absorption and Theatricality: Painting and Beholder in the Age of Diderot,* Berkeley, Los Angeles and London 1980. Perhaps Turner's most extreme example of inviting the viewer to participate in a painting is 'Regulus' (fig.87), in which the viewer takes the role of Regulus himself. On the viewer's relationship with this work (in which there is in fact very little foreground) see Paulson 1982, pp.81–2 and Nicholson 1990, pp.114–15 and p.139, n.51 in which some of the earlier literature is reviewed.

68   Routes to follow within a picture is another subject too vast to consider here. See Paulson 1982, Barrell 1980, and Wilton 1986 for an indication of the varied ways in which the subject may be approached.

69   This distinction has important implications. As a single example: Michael Kitson noted that Turner's 'Festival upon the Opening of the Vintage at Macon' (B&J 47) has a higher viewpoint than its Claudian model (Michael Kitson, 'Turner and Claude', *Turner Studies,* vol.2, no.2, Winter 1983, p.7). But Kitson was thinking only of the distant view (for which the vantage point is certainly higher) and not the immediate foreground relationship between the spectator and the picture. See also John Barrell, *The Idea of Landscape and the Sense of Place, 1730–1840,* Cambridge 1972, e.g. pp.6–27, and Barrell 1980, pp.153–4. For a further discussion of the possible significance of large foregrounds in early nineteenth-century British art see John Murdoch, 'Foregrounds and Focus: Changes in the Perception of Landscape c.1800' in *The Lake District: A Sort of National Property,* papers presented to a symposium at the Victoria and Albert Museum, 20–2 Oct. 1984. Published by the Countryside Commission and the V&A, 1986 (CCP 194).

70   Ruskin 1903–12, vol.4, p.88.
71   MS L f.7r.
72   MS BB f.35r.
73   Malton 1775, p.90.
74   MS L f.12r, building on Malton 1775, pp.29–30. Malton does mention Newton, but actually attributes the idea to Smith and Emerson, two eighteenth-century writers on optics.
75   Malton 1775, p.11. It should be noted that some eighteenth-century works on optics did discuss the idea: see Norman Daniels, *Thomas Reid's Inquiry: The Geometry of Visibles and the Case for Realism,* New York 1974, e.g. pp.5–6.
76   MS L f.15r. This is part of Turner's investigation of marginal distortion – see discussion of lecture 2 in chap.2, above.
77   MS D ff.8v–9r (earlier version of MS L). Note that alternative punctuation could give a different reading of the passage. (As in all quotations from Turner's lecture manuscripts given here, the punctuation is an editorial addition.)
78   On Parsey and Herdman, see Kemp (n.54 above).
79   MS L f.12v.
80   For example, the foreground paving in 'Hero and Leander' (fig.97) curves, particularly at the right-hand side, presumably to strengthen depth and the viewer's engagement with the picture. However, in this, and in other examples, it is often impossible to be certain whether the original line itself was in fact curved.
81   The main recent literature on the painting is Gage 1969, pp.93–5; Butlin and Joll; Powell 1987, pp.110–17; Mordechai Omer, 'Turner and "The Building of the Ark" from Raphael's Third Vault of the Loggia', *Burlington Magazine,* vol.117, no.872, Nov. 1975, pp.694–702; Gerald Finley, 'J.M.W. Turner's "Rome from the Vatican": A Palimpsest of History?', *Zeitschrift für Kunstgeschichte,* vol.49, 1986, pp.55–72; and McVaugh 1987. The latter two are exhaustive accounts of the painting. The anachronisms include the fact that Bernini's colonnades were built long after Raphael's death, although Raphael is present in the painting (also see below, esp. n.90), and that some of the easel paintings displayed were in fact frescoes – see Omer, p.694. Powell 1987, p.113 suggests: 'one reason behind the spatial peculiarities ... could well be that it was executed at great speed'. She feels that Turner's possible experiments with perspective in the picture 'did not succeed' (p.110). See also McVaugh, p.370.

82   See Roger Jones and Nicholas Penny, *Raphael,* New Haven and London 1983, p.194. The perspective skill with which the loggia was decorated may have encouraged Turner to experiment with perspective in his own painting. The loggia's early nineteenth-century reputation can be judged from the entry on panoramas in the 1824 supplement to the *Encyclopaedia Brittanica* in which its 'architectural representations and ornaments' are given as an example of this kind of depiction which 'comprehend ... the whole visible hemisphere, and sometimes nearly the whole sphere of vision' (p.108). For Turner's opinions about panoramas see below. For a modern account of the loggia perspective see Kemp 1990, p.70.

83   The curving in this painting means that analysis of the perspective geometry's precision is an even more risky undertaking than usual. Nevertheless, it is worth doing to show how closely Turner retained many of the broad principles of standard perspective. For example, not only does the horizon height of the architecture closely match that of the landscape horizon, but the horizon falls in the middle of the second floor of the Pontifical Palace block at the left. This is exactly as it should, for the loggia, where the artist/viewer stands and looks out, is also on the second floor of the palace.

84   McVaugh 1987, p.373 suggests that in view of the unusual technique of fig.114, with its extensive use of ink over pencil, Turner may have 'clarified it with pen' later. The drawing is now in bad condition, but the pencil underdrawing that is still visible does not conflict with the ink in terms of the establishment of the unusual picture space.

85   Generally it is assumed that this view is taken from the first bay. However, as Turner himself warned in his first perspective lecture (see chap.2, above), in some views it is simply not possible to determine how many columns (or pillars) lie behind the one that is shown in a picture, so the view could be from a different bay.

86   The huge scale of the architectural decoration at the left makes it absolutely clear that the viewpoint is to that side and not the other. It has to be between the pier that closes the left-hand margin and the vanishing point of the opposing palace block. The steep foreshortening of the landscape painting and the large scale of the fruit is consistent with a viewpoint in this area. It is not possible (or appropriate) to specify the viewpoint with greater accu-

87 P.G. Hamerton, *The Life of J.M.W. Turner RA*, 1895, p.171, quoted by Powell 1987, p.110.

88 The angle of view comprised in the finished picture is in the region of 140 degrees (see fig.115). This is remarkably wide (see n.63). For a viewer to see the painting under the same angle would require a viewing distance of only about one foot six inches. However, this does not take account of the twisted space of the picture. A further question is: should it be viewed with one eye or two, and should the head be kept still or moved? There is of course, no 'correct' way to view it, but the all-embracing effect is much more powerful if only one eye is used and the head is kept still (although the eye itself free to move – as in a standard perspective construction). In fact, it is unlikely that a flat painting could ever fill a two-eyed field of view completely, as it extends to 180 degrees (see n.63).

89 This study is not universally regarded as being of the loggia. Powell 1987, pp.117–18 describes it as a compositional sketch on the theme of an artist at work 'in a vaulted room'. However, McVaugh 1987, p.372 does see it as being a compositional sketch of Raphael in the loggia, he also discusses its similarities to the oil on p.384; Finley (n.81), p.58 also sees the study as the loggia; he also discusses it in some detail, including the picture space. There is a further 'compositional study' (TB CLXXIX 25v); this is also discussed in detail by both Finley and McVaugh.

90 My feeling is that the differences in scale mean that the figure scene is not intended to be 'real' in time and place: it is a dream, or a play, or an arrangement of porcelain figures. Raphael has stepped (in time and space) from his plinth at the end of the loggia and come to act out a scene on a stage. Other possibilities are explored in much more detail in the literature (see n.81 for references).

91 Comprehensive details of the visit and the work Turner produced in connection with it are given in Gerald Finley, *Turner and George IV in Edinburgh, 1822*, 1981.

92 MS L f.16r.

93 MS D f.9r (early version of MS L f.16r). Unfortunately Turner's argument becomes hard to follow (and a possibly crucial passage on MS L f.16r has faded to the point of illegibility). The passage continues, to talk of 'the retina of the eye being a parabola … and receiving in a circle all objects; produced at the point of intersection a parabolic curve'. This is then related to marginal distortion and other 'fallacies of vision'. For more information about panoramas in early nineteenth-century London see Ralph Hyde, *Panoramania!*, exh. cat., Barbican Art Gallery 1988. Turner and panorama is discussed briefly on p.29 of that catalogue.

94 For the history of this work, and others related to it, see Martin Butlin, Mollie Luther and Ian Warrell, *Turner at Petworth: Painter and Patron*, 1989, esp. pp.71–7, to which I am indebted for much of the information that follows.

95 The ratio of width to height of the three sketchbook pages taken together is about 5:1; that of the oil is about 2.3:1.

96 The authors of *Turner and Petworth* (n.94) do not relate any of the gouache studies directly to the oil. They also treat fig.126 as a sketch for a different Petworth picture (p.75). In a useful discussion on p.138 (n.10), further pencil sketches related to the picture are identified and it is noted that one of these condenses part of the view in the sketchbook. It is almost certainly impossible to establish the exact sequence in which the various works were made and they have been presented here primarily to indicate the extent of the view that Turner incorporated in the painting, rather than the way in which he developed the design of the picture.

97 See, for example, cat.no.5 in Powell 1991. The pencil sketches are in a ratio of about 9:1, but the finished work is in the ratio 1.8:1 – five times narrower. For further examples of compression of wide sketches into narrow pictures see Finley 1980, pp.109–16 and pp.132–3 and cat.nos.50 and 54 of Diane Perkins, *Turner: The Third Decade: Watercolours 1810–1820*, exh. cat., Tate Gallery 1990.

98 Wallace 1979 identifies eleven works that are on square canvases and framed as squares, quasi-octagons or circles. More details are given below in n.105.

99 For circular bounds to the vertical field of view, see, for example, Charles Hayter, *An Introduction to Perspective Drawing and Painting*, 1815, p.68 and Anon., *The Artists Repository*, 1808, vol.2, p.52. The *field* of view can be conceived as slightly irregular, and bounded partly by, for example, the top lip and eyebrows; it is then distinguished from the *visual world* which extends to a full 360 degrees in all directions. See, for example, James J. Gibson, *The Perception of the Visual World*, Cambridge Mass., 1950, esp. pp.27–9.

100 Ruskin, 1903–12, vol.1, p.236. See also Kemp (n.54). The reasons for the inclusion of Ruskin's paper in the Repton book is connected to the fact that it was published by J.J. Loudon, who also published the *Architectural Magazine*. For Ruskin's error see n.63 above.

101 Ibid. p.241.

102 Ruskin tells us this in an article published in 1838. See Ruskin 1903–12, vol.1, p.231.

103 Ibid., p.242. Here, Ruskin singles out for praise 'Copley Fielding's management of the angles of a breezy sea-piece'.

104 See the entry for 'Light and Colour' in Butlin and Joll (no.405). Also see the entry for 'Undine Giving the Ring to Massaniello' (no.424).

105 According to Wallace 1979, 'Bacchus and Ariadne' (B&J 382) was probably exhibited in a circular frame in 1840. Butlin and Joll say it was probably finished in a circular frame. 'Dawn of Christianity' and 'Glaucus and Scylla' (B&J 394 and 395) were exhibited in circular frames in 1841. 'Peace – Burial at Sea' and 'War. The Exile and the Rock Limpet' (B&J 399 and 400) were both exhibited in quasi-octagons in 1842; and figs.132 and 133 (B&J 404 and 405) exhibited in quasi-octagons in 1843. 'Undine Giving the Ring to Massaniello' (B&J 424) and 'The Angel Standing in the Sun' (fig.134, B&J 425), exhibited in square frames in 1846. Holcomb 1970, p.27 notes the circular brushwork of the corners, but describes it as 'informal', whereas it in fact seems to have a firm theoretical basis.

106 A further question that can be raised in this context is that of Turner's eyesight. Contemporary critics often attributed Turner's effects to eye problems (see, e.g. B&J 395), as did a paper of the 1870s by R. Liebreich (opthalmic surgeon and lecturer at St Thomas's Hospital), see Patrick Trevor Roper, *The World through Blunted Sight*, 1990 ed., pp.92–3.

107 For a useful discussion of the context from which Turner's vignettes develop see Cecilia Powell, 'Turner's Vignettes and the Making of Rogers's *Italy*', *Turner Studies*, vol.3, no.1, Summer 1983, pp.2–13. Also see Holcomb 1969 and Holcomb 1970. Suggestions for the origins of Turner's vortices have been many and varied. For a summary of some of them see Paulson 1982, esp. pp.98 *et seq*. Paulson himself argues at some length that the vortex had origins for Turner in the twisting, *turning* barber's pole of his father; it is therefore a play on Turner's own name. To this imaginative suggestion one might reply to Paulson, of course entering Turner's London (but not strictly Cockney, for you cannot hear the bells of St Mary-le-Bow from Maiden Lane) idiom: 'You, *son*, must be *paul*ing my leg.'

108 Holcomb 1970, p.17, talking specifically of Turner's vignette of Fingal's Cave. Murdoch (n.69) p.54 talks of the role of the vignette earlier in the nineteenth century in similar terms. He argues that London watercolourists held the view that 'the eye works with a relatively small depth of field, and that the periphery of vision fades off into indistinctness. The vignette was seen to represent this effect accurately and therefore to offer superior "naturalism" of perception.' In general Holcomb says the vignette is 'a form which does not imply a window onto space, but is created by the relative emergence of forms from an indeterminate matrix' (Holcomb 1970, p.17) – I think I prefer Landseer's approach (n.109), below!

109 Finley 1980, p.44, n.14 notes that John Landseer, *Lectures on Engraving*, 1807, p.257

says that vignettes are a form in which to create 'a sort of midsummer-night's dream where fancy, unrestrained by time and place, indulges in the revelry of fairy fiction'.
110 Ruskin, 1903–12, vol.1, p.233. Kemp 1990, p.243 mistakenly extends Ruskin's point about the corners of rectangular pictures to Turner's vignettes.
111 Ruskin, 1903–12, vol.1, p.244.
112 Wilton 1986, p.420 notes Turner's tendency to impose a central composition 'on many scenes that did not lend themselves obviously to such treatment'. Lawrence Gowing, *Turner: Imagination and Reality*, exh. cat., Museum of Modern Art, New York 1966, p.27 writes that many of Turner's later pictures are 'balanced on an incandescent central axis'. Wallace 1979 and Paulson 1982 also discuss the centrality of many of Turner's later works. Wallace (pp.109–10) even sees 'Rome from the Vatican' (fig.112) as a centralised composition.
113 For example in 'Regulus' (fig.87) where Turner ruled lines to mark the edge of the rays of light from the sun. See Wilton 1986, p.418. I share much of Wilton's view that 'the brilliance of the sunlight does ... dissolve and obliterate forms ... Even so ... Turner needed to feel the space within which his light operated in terms of an absolutely architectural system of perspective.' See also n.120, below. Paulson goes further and argues that in many pictures, including 'Regulus', 'The sun's shape and the shape of its emanations come to determine the shape of the composition, and then the shape of the canvas itself, replacing the normal rectangle of a landscape with a circle' (Paulson 1982, p.83). See also Holcomb 1970, pp.27–8 where the author argues that Turner's vortices are 'virtually a symbol' for his 'preoccupation with the primacy of light'.
114 Finley 1980, p.160 describes Turner's vignettes as 'centrifugal', but he also notes their spatial organisation. Turner's vortical compositions are generally seen as anti-classical. Paulson 1982, p.73 argues that Turner replaced 'box perspective with the vortex as the defining structure of unity in time and space'. See also Karl Kroeber, 'Romantic Historicism: The Temporal Sublime' in *Images of Romanticism*, ed. Karl Kroeber and William Walling, New Haven and London 1978, pp.163–4. Holcomb 1970, p.16 talks of anti-classical compositions in Turner. She claims the series of pictures of the 1840s features a 'loss of spatial reference' (p.28). Holcomb 1969 identifies many classical elements in Turner's vignettes for the 1830 edition of Rogers's *Italy* and distinguishes them from later works. Jonathan Crary, *Techniques of the Observer: On Vision and Modernity in the Nineteenth Century*, Cambridge, Mass. and London 1990, pp.139–41 treats Turner's vortical paintings as complete alternatives to standard perspective. In 'Light and Colour' (fig.133), 'the collapse of the older model of representation is complete: the view of the sun that had dominated so many of Turner's previous images now becomes a fusion of eye and sun ... If the circular structure of this painting and others of the same period mimic the shape of the sun, they also correspond with the pupil of the eye and the retinal field on which the temporal experience of an afterimage unfolds. Through the afterimage the sun is made to belong to the body.'
115 Norman Bryson, 'Enhancement and Displacement in Turner', *Essays on British Narrative Art, The Huntington Library Quarterly*, vol.49, no.1, Winter 1986, p.50.
116 MS Q f.4v.
117 MS M f.23r. Turner's depiction of aerial perspective (and his extremely brief coverage of it in his lectures) is a quite separate study to his use of linear perspective. Ruskin wrote much about it, and, as early as 1816, Hazlitt wrote that Turner painted 'representations not properly of the objects of nature as of the medium through which they were seen' (quoted in Paulson 1982, p.95).
118 MS M f.23r.
119 MS H f.15r.
120 Wilton 1986, p.418: 'Light itself obeys the laws of perspective and imposes a geometrical order on space.' See also n.113 above.
121 Kroeber (n.114) disagrees; he argues that for Turner 'colour ... is the antagonist of fixed forms. To structure a painting by colour ... is to organise by dissolving, diffusing and dissipating forms. It is to arrange according to the ever-changing dynamics of liquid or gaseous conditions, [and] dynamics irreducible to the definite boundaries of geometric shapes' (p.163). See also Wilton 1986, p.409.
122 Ruskin 1903–12, vol.16, p.33 (letter of 27 Nov. 1843).

GLOSSARY

ANGULAR PERSPECTIVE The use of standard perspective *(q.v.)* to depict straight lines that are not parallel or perpendicular to the picture plane.

APPEARANCE Artists see the appearance of an object with their 'common sense' perception. Thomas Malton Senior calls this the 'true appearance' of an object. It is distinct from the perspective representation of an object. See p.41.

APPARENT DIAMETER When a sphere is viewed its apparent diameter is seen, rather than its full diameter. See pp.39–40.

CENTRE See perspective centre point.

CURVILINEAR PERSPECTIVE The use of standard perspective *(q.v.)* to depict curvilinear forms and lines. See p.38.

DISTANCE POINTS Points on the horizon line the same distance from the perspective centre point *(q.v.)* as the artist is. The distance points are the vanishing points *(q.v.)* of horizontal lines at forty-five degrees to the picture plane.

EYE/DISTANCE POINT The point on the picture surface vertically above the perspective centre point *(q.v.)* that represents the artist's eye. It is the same distance from the centre as the distance points *(q.v.)*.

FRONTAL An object is frontal if one of its major faces is parallel to the picture plane.

HORIZON/HORIZONTAL LINE The line on the surface of the picture at the same height as the artist's eye.

MEASURE POINT METHOD A perspective method in which measurements of the object being depicted are marked off to scale on the picture surface and points representing the distance of the vanishing points from the eye are used.

ONE-POINT PERSPECTIVE The same as parallel perspective *(q.v.)*.

PARALLEL PERSPECTIVE The use of standard perspective *(q.v.)* to depict rectangular objects that are frontal *(q.v.)* to the picture plane.

PERSPECTIVE CENTRE POINT The point on the picture surface directly opposite the artist's eye; not necessarily the picture's physical centre. The perspective centre point is the vanishing point *(q.v.)* of horizontal lines perpendicular to the picture plane. See p.64.

RECTILINEAR PERSPECTIVE The use of standard perspective *(q.v.)* to represent straight lines. Note that Turner often uses the term as analogous to standard perspective.

STANDARD PERSPECTIVE 'Conventional', 'canonical' or 'traditional' linear perspective in which there is a single fixed viewpoint and lines that are straight in real life are represented by lines that are straight on the picture surface. Geometrically equivalent to the tracing on a window pane of the view through the window from a single fixed point. See p.17.

TWO-POINT PERSPECTIVE The same as angular perspective.

VANISHING POINT Any point on the picture surface where the perspective representations of two or more lines that are parallel in real life, meet.

VIEWPOINT In standard perspective, the point where the artist's single eye was located. Also the point from which a spectator should view the finished picture with one eye, in order to see the same scene (in linear terms) that the artist saw. See p.17.

NOTE
Some of the terms presented above are used with a variety of meanings in works on perspective. The explanations given here refer only to the way in which the terms are used throughout this book.

SELECT BIBLIOGRAPHY

This bibliography concentrates on those works referred to in abbreviated form in the notes, together with a few other items directly concerning Turner's lectures. References cited in full in the notes are not repeated here.

The best introductions to perspective are Kemp 1990 and B.A.R. Carter, 'Perspective', in Harold Osborne (ed.), *The Oxford Companion to Art*, Oxford 1970, pp.840–61. Turner's discussion of linear perspective in his lectures is the subject of my forthcoming PhD thesis *J.M.W. Turner's Approach to Perspective in his Royal Academy Lectures of 1811*, Courtauld Institute of Art, University of London.

All books are published in London unless otherwise stated.

Barrell, John, *The Dark Side of the Landscape: The Rural Poor in English Painting 1730–1840*, Cambridge 1980

Butlin, Martin and Joll, Evelyn, *The Paintings of J.M.W. Turner*, revised ed., New Haven and London 1984

Edwards, Edward, *A Practical Treatise of Perspective on the Principles of Dr Brook Taylor*, 1803

Euclid's Elements of Geometry, ed. Samuel Cunn, 8th ed., 1759

Farington, Joseph, *The Diary of Joseph Farington*, ed. Kenneth Garlick, Angus McIntyre, Kathryn Cave, New Haven and London 1978–84

Finberg, Alexander J., *A Complete Inventory of the Drawings of the Turner Bequest*, 1909

Finley, Gerald, *Landscapes of Memory: Turner as Illustrator to Scott*, 1980

Gage, John, *Colour in Turner: Poetry and Truth*, 1969

Gage, John, *J.M.W. Turner: 'A Wonderful Range of Mind'*, New Haven and London 1987

Hagen, Margaret A., *Varieties of Realism: Geometries of Representational Art*, Cambridge 1986

Holcomb, Adele M., 'A Neglected Classical Phase of Turner's Art: His Vignettes to Rogers's *Italy*', *Journal of the Warburg and Courtauld Institutes*, vol.32, 1969, pp.405–10

Holcomb, Adele M., 'The Vignette and the Vortical Composition in Turner's Oeuvre', *Art Quarterly*, 1970, vol.32, no.1, 1970, pp.16–29

Kemp, Martin, *The Science of Art*, New Haven and London 1990

Kirby, John Joshua, *Dr Brook Taylor's Method of Perspective Made Easy*, 1st London ed., 1765

Lamy, Bernard, *Perspective Made Easie*, 2nd English ed., 1710

London, Tate Gallery, *J.M.W.T. P.P [Professor of Perspective]* exh. leaflet, 1980

MacColl, D.S., 'Turner's Lectures at the Academy', *Burlington Magazine*, vol.12. 1907–8, pp.343–6

MacColl, D.S. 'A lecture by J.M.W. Turner on Landscape', *Artwork*, vol.5, 1929, pp.90–4

Malton, James, *The Young Painter's Maulstick, Being a Practical Treatise on Perspective*, 1800

Malton, Thomas [Senior], *A Compleat Treatise on Perspective in Theory and Practice on the Principles of Dr. Brook Taylor*, 1775

Malton, Thomas [Senior], *An Appendix, or Second Part, to the Compleat Treatise on Perspective*, 1783

McVaugh, Robert E., 'Turner and Rome, Raphael and the Fornarina', *Studies in Romanticism*, no.26, Fall 1987, pp.365–97

Nicholson, Kathleen, *Turner's Classical Landscapes: Myth and Meaning*, Princeton and Oxford 1990

Paulson, Ronald, *Literary Landscape: Turner and Constable* New Haven and London 1982

Powell, Cecilia, *Turner in the South: Rome, Naples, Florence*, New Haven and London 1987

Powell, Cecilia, *Turner's Rivers of Europe: The Rhine, Meuse and Mosel*, exh. cat., Tate Gallery 1991

Puttfarken, Thomas, 'From Central Perspective to Central Composition: The Significance of the Centric Ray,' *Marburger Jahrbuch für Kunstwissenschaft*, vol.21, 1986

Ruskin, John, *The Works of John Ruskin*, Library Edition, ed. E.T. Cook and A. Wedderburn, 1903–12

Shanes, Eric, *Turner's Human Landscape*, 1990

Taylor, Brook, *Linear Perspective*, 1715

Taylor, Brook, *Linear Perspective*, 2nd ed., 1719

Wallace, Marcia Briggs, 'J.M.W. Turner's Circular, Octagonal and Square Paintings 1840–1846', *Arts Magazine*, vol.53, no.8, April 1979, pp.107–17

Whitley, W.T., 'Turner as a Lecturer', *Burlington Magazine*, vol.22, 1913, pp.202–8, 255–9

Whitley, W.T., *Collected Papers*, British Museum Department of Prints and Drawings

Wilton, Andrew, *Turner and the Sublime*, exh. cat., British Museum 1980

Wilton, Andrew, 'Turner at Bonneville', *Essays in Honor of Paul Mellon*, John Wilmerding ed., Washington D.C. 1986

Wilton, Andrew, *Painting and Poetry: Turner's 'Verse Book' and his Work of 1804–1812*, exh. cat., Tate Gallery 1990

Ziff, Jerrold, '"Backgrounds: Introduction of Architecture and Landscape": A Lecture by J.M.W. Turner', *Journal of the Warburg and Courtauld Institutes*, vol.26, 1963, pp.124–47

Ziff, Jerrold, 'Turner, the Ancients, and the Dignity of the Art', *Turner Studies*, vol.3, no.2, Winter 1984, pp.45–52

Ziff, Jerrold, 'Turner as a Defender of the Art between 1810–1820', *Turner Studies*, vol.8, no.2, Winter 1988, pp.13–25

LIST OF WORKS

All works are by J.M.W. Turner unless otherwise stated. Catalogue numbers up to no.136 correspond to the figure numbers used in the text. Works shown in the exhibition are indicated with an asterisk. Dimensions are given in centimetres, followed by inches in brackets, height before width.

1 Manuscript of one of Turner's perspective lectures, after 1816
Private Collection

2 GEORGE SCHARF I
'Westmacott's Lecture on Sculpture at the Royal Academy, Somerset House'* c.1830
Lithograph on paper 26.5 × 35.5 (10$^{7/16}$ × 13$^{15/16}$)
Guildhall Library, Corporation of London

3 'The Geometry of Standard Perspective as the Intersection of the Cone of Vision', lecture diagram*
c.1816–28
Pencil and watercolour on paper 48.2 × 60.2 (19 × 23$^{3/4}$)
TB CXCV 2
D16971

4 A standard perspective representation as an intersection of the cone of vision (modern diagram)

5 *Perspective* sketchbook
'Dürer's Perspective Fenestre' (taken from Salomon de Caus, *La perspective avec la raison des ombres et mirroirs*, 1612, Tenth Theorem) c.1809
Pen and ink on paper 8.8 × 11.5 (3$^{1/2}$ × 4$^{1/2}$)
TB CVIII f.3 verso
D07360

6 'Guidobaldo del Monte's Perspective Method for a Cube', lecture diagram 29* (taken from fig.7) c.1810
Pencil and watercolour on paper 67.2 × 99.9 (26$^{1/2}$ × 39$^{3/8}$)
TB CXCV 73
D17043

7 Guidobaldo del Monte, *Perspectivae*, Pesaro 1600, p.135*
The British Library
Press mark c.78 c.8 (1–2)

8 *Perspective* sketchbook
Turner's copy of fig.7* c.1809
Pen and ink on paper 8.8 × 11.5 (3$^{1/2}$ × 4$^{1/2}$)
TB CVIII f.43
D07427

9 'Triangles within Circles', lecture diagram* (from *Euclid's Elements of Geometry*, ed. Samuel Cunn, 1759, book 4, proposition 5) c.1817–28
Watercolour on paper 58.4 × 87.4 (23 × 34$^{3/8}$)
TB CXCV 33
D17003

10 'Colour Circle No.1', lecture diagram* c.1822–8
Pencil and watercolour on paper 55.6 × 76.2 (21$^{7/8}$ × 30)
TB CXCV 178
D17149

11 'Interior of a Prison', lecture diagram 65* c.1810
Gouache, pencil and watercolour on paper 48.7 × 68.7 (19$^{1/8}$ × 27)
TB CXCV 120
D17090

12 'Interior of a Prison', lecture diagram 66* c.1810
Pencil and ink on paper 44.3 × 59.5 (17$^{7/16}$ × 23$^{3/8}$)
TB CXCV 121
D17091

13 'Interior of Brocklesby Mausoleum', lecture diagram 76 c.1810
Pencil and watercolour on paper 64 × 49 (25$^{1/4}$ × 19$^{1/4}$)
TB CXCV 130
D17101

14 'The "Temple of Neptune" at Paestum', lecture diagram* c.1810
Pencil and watercolour on paper 47.9 × 62.1 (18$^{7/8}$ × 24$^{1/2}$)
TB CXCV 102
D17072

15 JOHN LINNELL (1792–1882)
'Study of Turner's Father and Turner's Eyes while Lecturing, 27 January 1812'* 1812
Pencil on paper 18.7 × 22.5 (7$^{3/8}$ × 8$^{7/8}$)
T03117

16 'Cross-sections of the Human Body', lecture diagram 1, (after Dürer)*
c.1810
Watercolour on paper 61.8 × 79.7 (24$^{3/8}$ × 31$^{3/8}$)
TB CXCV 164
D17135

17 'Trajan's Column', lecture diagram 5
c.1810
Pencil and watercolour on paper 98 × 64.2 (38$^{5/8}$ × 25$^{1/4}$)
TB CXCV 153
D17124

18 'The Monument', lecture diagram 4*
c.1810
Pencil and watercolour on paper 67.5 × 101.1 (26$^{5/8}$ × 39$^{3/4}$)
TB CXCV 151
D17122

19 *Windmill and Lock* sketchbook
Notes about viewing the Monument*
c.1809
Pencil on paper 8.7 × 22.6 (3$^{3/8}$ × 8$^{7/8}$)
TB CXIV ff.12 verso, 13
D07977, 07978

20 'St George's, Bloomsbury', lecture diagram 6 c.1810
Pencil and watercolour on paper 74.2 × 46.7 (29$^{1/4}$ × 18$^{3/8}$)
TB CXCV 144
D17115

21 'Carlton House', lecture diagram*
c.1810
Pen and ink, watercolour on paper 68.4 × 139.2 (26$^{7/8}$ × 54$^{3/4}$)
TB CXCV 148
D17119

22 'The Admiralty', lecture diagram 10* (see also fig.23) c.1810
Pencil and watercolour on paper 78.2 × 132.8 (30$^{3/4}$ × 52)
TB CXCV 173
D17144

23 'The Proportion and Design of Raphael's "Transfiguration"', lecture diagram 10* (see also fig.22) c.1810
Pencil and watercolour on paper 76.3 × 55 (30 × 21$^{5/8}$)
TB CXCV 163
D17134

24 'Spheres at Different Distances from the Eye', lecture diagram 11* (after Thomas Malton, *A Compleat Treatise on Perspective*, 1775, pl.1, fig.3) *c*.1810
Pen and ink, watercolour on paper
48.5 × 60.2 (19$^{1}/_{8}$ × 23$^{3}/_{4}$)
TB CXCV 174
D17145

25 'Objects Above, Level with and Below the Eye', lecture diagram 13 (after Giovanni Paolo Lomazzo, *A Tracte Containing the Artes of Curious Paintinge, Carvinge and Buildinge*, English trans. R. Haydocke, Oxford 1598, book 5, p.204) *c*.1810
Pen and ink, watercolour on paper
48 × 60 (18$^{7}/_{8}$ × 23$^{5}/_{8}$)
TB CXCV 57
D17027

26 'The Terminology of Perspective of Joseph Moxon', lecture diagram 14* *c*.1810
Pen and ink, watercolour on paper
48.2 × 60 (19 × 23$^{5}/_{8}$)
TB CXCV 58
D17028

27 'The Terminology of Perspective of Brook Taylor', lecture diagram 15 *c*.1810
Watercolour on paper
67.7 × 101.5 (26$^{5}/_{8}$ × 40)
TB CXCV 59
D17029

28 'The Terminology of Perspective of Thomas Malton Junior', lecture diagram 16, later renumbered 47 *c*.1810
Watercolour on paper 67.5 × 100.2 (26$^{5}/_{8}$ × 39$^{1}/_{2}$)
TB CXCV 94
D17064

29 'Conic and Cylindrical Sections', lecture diagram 19 (after Thomas Malton, *A Compleat Treatise on Perspective*, 1775, figs.27–9, pl.7) *c*.1810
Watercolour on paper 67.4 × 99.9 (26$^{1}/_{2}$ × 39$^{3}/_{8}$)
TB CXCV 62
D17032

30 'The Geometry of a Parabola', lecture diagram 23 (after John Hamilton, *Stereography*, 1738, fig.84, no.1) *c*.1810
Pen and ink, pencil on paper
68.3 × 49.1 (26$^{7}/_{8}$ × 19$^{3}/_{8}$)
TB CXCV 67
D17037

31 'Real and Apparent Diameters of Spheres', lecture diagram 24 *c*.1810
Pen and ink, pencil on paper
66.8 × 99.1 (26$^{1}/_{4}$ × 39)
TB CXCV 68
D17038

32 Plan of the arrangement of the three-column problem (modern diagram)

33 The representation produced by the arrangement in fig.32 (modern diagram)

34 The effect of viewing fig.33 from correct and incorrect viewpoints (modern diagram)

35 'Analysis of the Perspective Representation of a Row of Pillars Parallel and Close to the Picture Plane', lecture diagram 25* *c*.1810
Pencil and watercolour on paper
66.8 × 99.5 (26$^{1}/_{4}$ × 39$^{1}/_{8}$)
TB CXCV 69
D17039

36 'Perspective Representation of a Row of Pillars and a Column Parallel and Close to the Picture Plane', lecture diagram* *c*.1810
Pencil and watercolour on paper
78 × 133.2 (30$^{3}/_{4}$ × 52$^{1}/_{2}$)
TB CXCV 146
D17117

37 'Perspective Method for a Square' (attributed by Turner to Viator (Jean Pelerin)), lecture diagram 27 *c*.1810
Pencil and watercolour on paper
67.2 × 99.9 (26$^{1}/_{2}$ × 39$^{3}/_{8}$)
TB CXCV 71
D17041

38 'Perspective Method by Andrea Pozzo', lecture diagram 34, (taken from John Joshua Kirby, *Dr Brook Taylor's Method of Perspective Made Easy*, 1768, book 2, pl.19, fig.6) *c*.1810
Pencil and watercolour on paper
67.2 × 99.8 (26$^{1}/_{2}$ × 39$^{1}/_{4}$)
TB CXCV 78
D17048

39 'Basic Perspective Method for a Rectangular Object', lecture diagram 35* *c*.1810
Pencil and watercolour on paper
67.2 × 99.8 (26$^{1}/_{2}$ × 39$^{1}/_{4}$)
TB CXCV 79
D17049

40 'Basic Perspective Construction of a House', lecture diagram 36* (see also fig.41) *c*.1810
Pencil and watercolour on paper
67.7 × 100.5 (26$^{5}/_{8}$ × 39$^{1}/_{2}$)
TB CXCV 80
D17050

41 'A House in Perspective', lecture diagram 36 (see also fig.40) *c*.1810
Watercolour over tracing on paper
49 × 69 (19$^{5}/_{16}$ × 27$^{3}/_{16}$)
TB CXCV 82
D17052

42 Turner's perspective construction of a house (fig.40) with correct standard perspective representation overlaid (modern diagram)

43 'Sirigatti's Method for a Tuscan Capital, and a Method for a Circle Attributed to Moxon and Androuet du Cerceau', lecture diagram 38* (partly from Lorenzo Sirigatti, *La pratica della prospettiva*, Venice 1596, pl.32) *c*.1810
Watercolour on paper 66.7 × 98.5 (26$^{1}/_{4}$ × 38$^{3}/_{4}$)
TB CXCV 85
D17055

44 'Tuscan Column in Perspective', lecture diagram 40 *c*.1810
Watercolour on paper 68.1 × 48.5 (26$^{3}/_{4}$ × 19$^{1}/_{8}$)
TB CXCV 88
D17058

45 Perspective Construction of a Tuscan Column', lecture diagram 41 *c*.1810
Pen and ink on paper 68 × 48.4 (26$^{3}/_{4}$ × 19)
TB CXCV 90
D17060

46 'Corinthian Capital in Perspective', lecture diagram 53 *c*.1810
Watercolour on paper 67.4 × 101 (26$^{1}/_{2}$ × 39$^{3}/_{4}$)
TB CXCV 103
D17073

47 'Perspective Construction of a Corinthian Capital', lecture diagram 54 *c*.1810
Pencil and watercolour on paper
67.8 × 99.5 (26$^{3}/_{4}$ × 39$^{1}/_{8}$)
TB CXCV 104
D17074

48 'Perspective Construction of Pulteney Bridge, Bath', lecture diagram 58*
c.1810
Pencil and watercolour on paper
67.4 × 100.6 (26½ × 41¾)
TB CXCV 113
D17083

49 'Pulteney Bridge, Bath, in Perspective', lecture diagram 59*
c.1810
Pencil and watercolour on paper
67.2 × 99.9 (26½ × 39⅜)
TB CXCV 114
D17084

50 Manuscript of first draft of lecture 5, studies of light reflected between adjacent plane surfaces* c.1809
Private Collection

51 'Reflections in a Single Polished Metal Globe and in a Pair of Polished Metal Globes', lecture diagram* c.1810
Oil and pencil on paper 64 × 96.8 (25¼ × 38⅛)
TB CXCV 176
D17147

52 'Reflections in a Transparent Globe', lecture diagram c.1810
Oil on paper 22 × 26.4 (8⅝ × 10⅜)
TB CXCV 177A
D17148

53 'Reflections and Refractions in Two Transparent Globes, One Half-filled with Water', lecture diagram* c.1810
Watercolour on paper 22.4 × 40 (8⅞ × 15¾)
TB CXCV 177C
D40025

54 RAPHAEL (1483–1520)
'Cartoon for the Tapestry of St Paul Preaching at Athens' c.1515–16
Gouache on paper 343.5 × 442 (135¼ × 174)
Her Majesty The Queen (on loan to the Victoria and Albert Museum)

55 'Geometry of the Figure of St Paul in Raphael's "St Paul Preaching at Athens"', lecture diagram c.1812–28
Watercolour on paper 58.6 × 71 (23⅛ × 28)
TB CXCV 168
D17139

56 MARTINO ROTA AFTER TITIAN
'The Martyrdom of St Peter' [n.d.]
Engraving 40 × 27.1 (15¾ × 10⅝)
Trustees of the British Museum, London

57 'Perspective Study of a Cross on a Cube', preparatory study for a lecture diagram* c.1810
Pen and ink, pencil on paper
38.5 × 54.4 (15⅛ × 21⅜)
TB CXCV 158
D17129

58 'Perspective Study of a Doric Entablature', preparatory study for lecture diagrams* c.1810
Pen and ink, pencil and watercolour on paper 30.6 × 48.8 (12 × 19¼)
TB CXCV 98
D17068

59 'Perspective Study of Pulteney Bridge, Bath', preparatory study for lecture diagrams* c.1810
Pen and ink, pencil on paper
37.6 × 54.6 (14¾ × 21½)
TB CXCV 111
D17081

60 'Pulteney Bridge, Bath in Perspective',* tracing from fig.59
c.1810
Tracing on paper 56 × 76 (22 × 29⅞)
TB CXCV 112
D17082

61 'Radley Hall'* 1789
Pen and ink, watercolour on paper
37.4 × 53.2 (14¾ × 21)
TB III C
D00048

62 'The Pantheon, Oxford Street, the Morning after the Fire' RA 1792
Pencil and watercolour on paper
51.6 × 64 (20¼ × 25¼)
TB IX A
W 27
D00121

63 'The Interior of the Hall of Christ Church, Oxford'* c.1798–1804
Pencil on paper 35.2 × 48.3 (13⅞ × 19)
TB L J
D02351

64 'The Interior of New College Chapel, Oxford'* c.1798–1801
Gouache, pencil and watercolour on paper 76.1 × 58.4 (30 × 23)
TB L F
D02347

65 'Cassiobury'* c.1807
Pen and ink on paper 33.9 × 74.2 (13⅜ × 29¼)
TB CXX A
D08241

66 'Ely Cathedral – The Interior of the Octagon'* 1794
Pencil on paper 78.2 × 59.3 (30¾ × 23⅜)
TB XXII P
D00369

67 'Mainz' ?1840
Gouache, pencil and watercolour on paper 19.4 × 28.3 (7⅝ × 11⅛)
TB CCCLXIV 293
D36150

68 'Promenade with Figures' after 1837
Gouache, pencil and watercolour on paper 34.3 × 50.9 (13½ × 20)
TB CCCLXV 24
D36314

69 'Entrance to the Little Chartreuse' 1802
Gouache and pencil on paper
21.9 × 28.5 (8⅝ × 11¼)
TB LXXIV 24
D04517

70 'Pass of Splügen' c.1841
Pencil and watercolour on paper
22.5 × 33 (8⅞ × 13)
TB CCCXXXVI 11
D33588

71 Perspective structure of figs.69–70 (modern diagram)

72 'The Road from Voreppe to Grenoble' 1802
Gouache and pencil on paper
21.5 × 28.5 (8⅛ × 11¼)
TB LXXIV 20
D04513

73 'Palazzo Tasca-Papafava, Venice' ?1840
Gouache and watercolour on paper
19.4 × 28.2 (7⅝ × 11⅛)
TB CCCXVII 31
D32216

74 Perspective structure of figs.72–3 (modern diagram)

75 'Bellinzona from the Road to Locarno' c.1841
Gouache, pencil and watercolour on paper 22.9 × 28.9 (9 × 11⅜)
TB CCCXXXII 25
D33495

76 Perspective structure of fig.75 (modern diagram)

77 'Calais Pier, with French Poissards Preparing for Sea: An English Packet Arriving' exh.1803
Oil on canvas 172 × 240
(67¾ × 94½)
Trustees of the National Gallery, London

78 'Frosty Morning' exh.1813
Oil on canvas 113.7 × 174.6
(44¾ × 68¾)
B&J 127
N00492

79 'Palestrina – Composition'* 1828
Oil on canvas 140.3 × 248.9
(55¼ × 98)
B&J 295
N06283

80 'Harfleur' c.1832
Gouache and watercolour on paper
13.8 × 18.7 (5⅜ × 7⅜)
TB CCLIX 86
D24651

81 'Bridge at Meulan' c.1832
Gouache and watercolour on paper
14.2 × 19.3 (5⅝ × 7⅝)
TB CCLIX 116
W 977
D24681

82 'Isis' 1819
Mezzotint on paper 18 × 26.1
(7⅛ × 10¼)
R L68
A01143

83 'Stangate Creek on the River Medway' c.1824
Watercolour on paper 16.2 × 24
(6⅜ × 9½)
TB CCVIII A
W 746
D18134

84 'Lausanne: Cathedral and Bridge'* 1841
Pencil and watercolour on paper
23.5 × 33.5 (9¼ × 13⅛)
TB CCCXXXV 26
D33566

85 'View across the Campagna with a Low Sun'* 1819
Gouache, pencil and watercolour on paper 25.2 × 40.4 (9⅞ × 15⅞)
TB CLXXXVII 43
D16131

86 'Figures in a Storm'* ?after 1830
Watercolour on paper 35.4 × 50.7
(14 × 20)
TB CCCLXV 25
D36315

87 'Regulus' 1828, reworked 1837
Oil on canvas 89.5 × 123.8
(35¼ × 48¾)
B&J 294
N00519

88 'Llandaff Cathedral: The West Front'* 1795–6
Pencil and watercolour on paper
35.5 × 25.9 (14 × 10¼)
TB XXVIII A
D00686

89 'Fonthill Abbey: South Front'* 1799
Pencil on paper 46.6 × 32.8
(18⅜ × 12⅞)
TB XLVII I
D02178

90 'Holy Island Cathedral'* 1808
Mezzotint on paper 18.1 × 25.9
(7⅛ × 10¼)
R LII
A00932

91 'The Ducal Palace: The Porta della Carta, Venice'* ?1833
Gouache, pencil and watercolour on paper 30.5 × 23.4 (12 × 9¼)
TB CCCXVIII 28
D32247

92 'St George's, Bloomsbury', lecture diagram 7* c.1810
Pencil and watercolour on paper
74.2 × 46.7 (29¼ × 18⅜)
TB CXCV 145
D17116

93 'The Grand Canal, Venice: The Rialto, the Palazzo Balbi on the Left'* ?1840
Pencil and watercolour on paper
22.3 × 32.8 (8¾ × 12⅞)
TB CCCXV 20
D32136

94 'Interior of the Great Room at Somerset House', lecture diagram 26,* c.1810
Pencil and watercolour on paper
66.9 × 100 (26⅜ × 39⅜)
TB CXCV 70
D17040

95 'Interior of Christ Church Cathedral, Oxford'* c.1799
Gouache, pen and ink, pencil, watercolour on paper 67.8 × 50.1
(26¾ × 19¾)
TB L G
D02348

96 'The Portico of St Peter's, Rome'* 1819
Gouache, pencil and watercolour on paper 36.8 × 23.2 (14½ × 9⅛)
TB CLXXXIX 6
D16332

97 'The Parting of Hero and Leander'* exh.1837
Oil on canvas 146.1 × 236.2
(57½ × 93)
B&J 370
L01408
Trustees of the National Gallery, on loan to the Tate Gallery

98 'Isola Bella, Lago Maggiore'* 1827
Watercolour, pencil and ink on paper
24.5 × 30.5 (9⅝ × 12)
TB CCLXXX 150
D27667

99 The effect of a close viewpoint and wide viewing angle shown from above (modern diagram)

100 Close viewpoint and wide viewing angle shown from one side (modern diagram)

101 'Mountains beside a Lake'* 1802
Chalk, gouache and pencil on paper
21.5 × 28.5 (8½ × 11¼)
TB LXXIV 49
D04542

102 'White Cliffs, Eu'* 1845
Pencil and watercolour on paper
23.1 × 32.7 (9⅛ × 12⅞)
TB CCCLIX 14
D35449

103 'Naples with Vesuvius'* 1819
Pencil on paper 25.6 × 40.5
(10⅛ × 16)
TB CLXXXVII 14
D16102

104 'St Anne's Hill II (In the Garden)'* c.1832
Pencil and watercolour on paper
24.4 × 30.8 (9⅝ × 12⅛)
TB CCLXXX 171
W 1201
D27688

105 'Forum Romanum, for Mr Soane's Museum' exh.1826
Oil on canvas 145.7 × 236.3
(57⅜ × 93⅛)
B&J 233
N00504

106 'Rouen Cathedral'* *c.*1832
Gouache and watercolour on paper
14 × 19.4 (5½ × 7⅝)
TB CCLIX 109
W 965
D24674

107 'Lausanne, Looking East'* 1841
Pen and ink, pencil and watercolour on paper 23.5 × 33.1 (9¼ × 13)
TB CCCXXXIV 3
D33527

108 'The Decline of the Carthaginian Empire'* exh.1817
Oil on canvas 170.2 × 238.8 (67 × 94)
B&J 135
N00499

109 CLAUDE LORRAIN
'Seaport: The Embarkation of St Ursula' 1641
Oil on canvas 113 × 149 (44½ × 58⅝)
Trustees of the National Gallery, London

110 'Town on the Loire', *c.*1832
Gouache, pen and ink and watercolour on paper 13 × 18.5 (5⅛ × 7¼)
TB CCLIX 204
D24769

111 'Saumur'* *c.*1832
Gouache, pen and ink and watercolour on paper 13.1 × 18.6 (5⅛ × 7⅜)
TB CCLIX 201
D24766

112 'Rome from the Vatican. Raffaelle, Accompanied by La Fornarina, Preparing his Pictures for the Decoration of the Loggia'* exh.1820
Oil on canvas 177.2 × 335.3 (69¾ × 132)
B&J 228
N00503

113 *Tivoli and Rome* sketchbook
Study for 'Rome from the Vatican'* 1819
Pencil on paper 11.2 × 18.3 (4⅜ × 7¼)
TB CLXXIX f.13 verso
D14955

114 Study for 'Rome from the Vatican'* 1819
Gouache, pen, pencil and watercolour on paper 23.3 × 37.1 (9⅛ × 14⅝)
TB CLXXXIX 41
D16368

115 Plan of the Vatican (modern diagram)

116 *Tivoli and Rome* sketchbook
Study for 'Rome from the Vatican' 1819
Pencil on paper 11.2 × 18.3 (4⅜ × 7¼)
TB CLXXIX f.26
D14972

117 *King's Visit to Edinburgh* sketchbook
Study for 'George IV at St Giles's, Edinburgh'* 1822
Pencil on paper 11.6 × 18.7 (4½ × 7⅜)
TB CC f.33 verso
D17559

118 *King's Visit to Edinburgh* sketchbook
Study for 'George IV at St Giles's, Edinburgh'* 1822
Pencil on paper 11.6 × 18.7 (4½ × 7⅜)
TB CC f.34
D17560

119 'George IV at St Giles's, Edinburgh'* *c.*1822
Oil on wood 74.6 × 91.8 (29⅜ × 36⅛)
B&J 247
N02857

120 Sketch of geometry of a panorama in endpapers of Turner's copy of Joseph Priestley, *A Familiar Introduction to the Theory and Practice of Perspective,* London 1770* *c.*1809–28
Private Collection

121 'Petworth Park: Tillington Church in the Distance'* *c.*1828
Oil on canvas 60 × 145.7 (23⅝ × 57⅜)
B&J 283
N00559

122 'Sunset across Petworth Park'* 1827
Gouache and watercolour on paper 14 × 19.3 (5½ × 7⅝)
TB CCXLIV 2
D22664

123 'Petworth Park: Sunset with a Cart' 1827
Gouache and watercolour on paper 13.7 × 18.7 (5⅜ × 7⅜)
Mint Museum of Art, Charlotte, North Carolina. The Harry and Mary Dalton Collection

124 *Petworth* sketchbook
'Petworth Park'* *c.*1827
Pencil on paper 11.4 × 37 (4½ × 14⅝)
TB CCXLIII ff.77 verso, 78
D22657, 22658

125 'Petworth Park'* *c.*1827
Pencil on paper 11.2 × 18.4 (4⅜ × 7¼)
TB CCCXLI 380
D34102

126 *Petworth* sketchbook
'Petworth Park' *c.*1827
Pencil on paper 11.4 × 37 (4½ × 14⅝)
TB CCXLIII ff.76 verso, 77
D22655, 22656

127 'Glade and Greensward'* 1827
Gouache and watercolour on paper 13.8 × 19.1 (5⅜ × 7½)
TB CCXLIV 105
D22767

128 'A View on the Rhine or Neckar'* 1840
Pencil and watercolour on paper 22.9 × 32.8 (9 × 12⅞)
TB CCCXLIX 27
D35151

129 'Dinant from the South-East: Evening' *c.*1839
Gouache, pen and ink, and watercolour on blue paper 13.9 × 19.1 (5½ × 7½)
TB CCXX T
D20227

130 'Goldau'* *c.*1842
Pencil and watercolour with pen on paper 22.8 × 29 (9 × 11³⁄₉)
TB CCCLXIV 281
D36131

131 AFTER J.M.W. TURNER
'Loch Coriskin'* 1834
Engraving on paper 8.1 × 13 (3¼ × 5⅛)
R 511
T04957

132 'Shade and Darkness – The Evening of the Deluge' exh.1843
Oil on canvas 78.7 × 78.1 (31 × 30¾)
B&J 404
N00531

133 'Light and Colour (Goethe's Theory) – the Morning after the Deluge – Moses Writing the Book of Genesis',* exh.1843
Oil on canvas 78.7 × 78.7 (31 × 31)
B&J 405
N00532

134 'The Angel Standing in the Sun', exh.1846
Oil on canvas 78.7 × 78.7 (31 × 31)
B&J 425
N00550

135 'The Evil Spirit'* c.1832
Pencil and watercolour on paper 24.4 × 31.1 (9⅝ × 12¼)
TB CCLXXX 202
W 1207
D27719

136 EDWARD GOODALL (1795–1870) AFTER J.M.W. TURNER
'The Fall of the Rebel Angels'* 1835
Line-engraving on paper 22 × 15.5 (8⅝ × 6⅛)
R 599
T06286

The following items are exhibited only and not illustrated in this book

137 *Greenwich* sketchbook
Notes about the perspective of Raphael's Tapestry Cartoons*
c.1809–10
7.6 × 11.5 (3 × 4½)
TB CII f.24 verso
D06767

138 *Frittlewell* sketchbook
Notes about Jan Vredeman de Vries *Perspective*, The Hague, 1604–5,*
c.1809–10
10.7 × 18 (4¼ × 7⅛)
TB CXII f.77 verso
D07835

139 'Holy Island Cathedral'* c.1807
Pen and ink and sepia wash on paper 18.3 × 26.2 (7¼ × 10¼)
TB CXVI N
D08115

140 'Ramsgate'* c.1825
Pencil and watercolour on paper 16 × 23.2 (6¼ × 9⅛)
TB CCVIII Q
D18150

141 'The Terrace at St Germain en Laye'* c.1830–1
Pen and ink, pencil and watercolour on paper 10 × 28.2 (4 × 11⅛)
TB CCLX 60
D24896

142 'Unidentified Cathedral'* after c.1830
Pencil on paper 19.6 × 14.6 (7¾ × 5¾)
TB CCLXI 39
D25011

143 'Cod on the Beach'* c.1835
Gouache, pencil and watercolour on paper 20.2 × 15.3 (8 × 6)
TB CCLXXX 4
D27521

144 'Study for Unidentified Vignette'* ?c.1826–36
Watercolour on paper 17.8 × 22.7 (7 × 9)
TB CCLXXX 65
D27582

145 'Martigny'* c.1827
Pencil and watercolour on paper 25.3 × 28.6 (10 × 11¼)
W 1159
TB CCLXXX 154
D27671

146 'Tornaro'* c.1832
Pencil and watercolour on paper 18.5 × 16 (7¼ × 6¼)
W 1185
TB CCLXXX 172
D27689

147 'Petworth Park'* c.1827
Pencil on paper 11.3 × 18.4 (4½ × 7¼)
TB CCCXLI 225
D33935

148 'Lausanne from the Walls'* 1842
Watercolour on paper 23.4 × 31.2 (9¼ × 12¼)
TB CCCLXIV 290
D36145

149 Earliest draft of a perspective lecture* c.1809
The British Library
ADD MS 46151 A ff.15 verso, 16 recto

150 Plan for first perspective lecture* c.1809
The British Library
ADD MS 46151 B f.3 verso

151 First full draft of first perspective lecture* c.1809
The British Library
ADD 46151 C ff.6 verso, 7 recto

152 Fine, 'Rolls', copy of first perspective lecture*
Copied by William Rolls 1810, revised by Turner 1810 onwards, possibly continuing as late as 1828
The British Library
ADD 46151 K ff.6 verso, 7 recto

153 Pages from Samuel Cunn, ed., *The Elements of Euclid*, 8th ed.*, 1759
Annotated by Turner, probably after 1814
The British Library
ADD 46151 V ff.21 verso, 22 recto

154 Letter to John Taylor, 16 January 1811*
The British Library
ADD MS 50118 f.23 recto

155 Admission ticket to Turner's first lecture of 10 January 1814, signed by Edward Bird RA*
Royal Academy of Arts

156 AFTER J.M.W. TURNER
'Smailholm Tower'* 1834
Line-engraving on paper 11 × 9.1 (4⅜ × 3⅝)
R 494
T05135

LENDERS

The British Library 7, 149–54
Guildhall Library, Corporation of London 2
Private Collection 50, 120
Royal Academy of Arts 155
(Numbers refer to the List of Works)

PHOTOGRAPHIC CREDITS

The British Library; The British Museum;
Guildhall Library; Mint Museum of Art,
Charlotte, North Carolina. The Harry
and Mary Dalton Collection; National
Gallery, London; Godfrey New
Photographics Ltd; Tate Gallery
Photographic Department;
V&A Picture Library

INDEX

All subject entries are listed under 'Turner, J.M.W.' or 'Perspective'

Accolti, Pietro 107 n.63
Adam, Robert 47
Alberti, Leon Baptista 17, 34
Aleaume, J. 107 n.63
Algarotti, Francesco 35, 104 n.20
Androuet du Cerceau, Jacques 45, 47 fig.43, 104 n.17, 107 n.63
Armstrong, Sir Walter 57, 103

Barbaro, Daniel 107 n.63
Bardwell, Thomas 104 n.8
Brunelleschi 34
Beaumont, Sir George 111 n.65

Caillebotte, Gustave 109 n.22
Canaletto 110 n.35, 44
Carracci 32
Cimabue 34
Clarke, Henry 104 n.7
Claude 74, 81 fig.109, 109 n.31, 110 n.35
Cunn, Samuel 23 fig.9

De Caus, Salomon 17 fig.5, 104 n.17, 107 nn.33, 63
Dubreuil, Jean 107 n.48
Du Fresnoy, Charles Alphonse 38–9
Dürer, Albrecht 17 fig.5, 31–2 fig.16, 34, 37, 44, 64, 104 n.17
Dyck, Sir Anthony van 51, 53

Edwards, Edward 64, 104 n.4, 110 n.35
Emerson, William 39
Euclid 23 fig.9, 37, 105 n.47, 110 n.60
Eyck, Jan van 34

Ferguson, James 104 n.14
Fielding, Anthony Vandyke Copley 112 n.103
Florentino, Stephano 34
Fry, Roger 28
Fuseli, Henry 26, 27

Gandy, Joseph Michael 104 n.4
Giulio Romano 109 n.30
Guidobaldo del Monte 19 figs.6–8, 107 n.63

Hamilton, John 39 fig.30, 104 n.14
Hardwick, Thomas 58
Hayter, Charles 104 n.7, 112 n.99
Herdman, William 84
Highmore, Joseph 41, 104 n.14

Junius, Franciscus 19, 32

Kata Phusin (John Ruskin) 98–9
Kirby, John Joshua 19, 41–2, 44 fig.38, 104 n.8, 105 n.47, 108 n.70

Lairesse, Gerard de 108 n.85
Lamy, Bernard 40–1, 104 n.14
Lautensack, Heinrich 107 n.63
Leonardo da Vinci 31, 40, 110 n.60
Linnell, John 27 fig.15
Lomazzo, Giovanni Paolo 37 fig.25, 106 n.4

Malton, James 15, 70, 104 n.14
Malton, Thomas (Junior) 15, 37, 38 fig.28, 47, 70, 71–2, 104 n.15
Malton, Thomas (Senior) 15, 19, 37 fig.24, 38, 39 fig.29, 39–40, 41–2, 70, 83–4, 107 n.27, 110 nn.44, 63
Marolois, Samuel 107 nn.62, 63
Michelangelo 31
Milton, John 100, 105 n.30
Moxon, Joseph 37 fig.25, 38 fig.26, 45, 47 fig.43, 107 n.63

Newton, Sir Isaac 84
Niceron, Jean Francois 107 n.63
Noble, Edward 41

Parsey, Arthur 84
Pelerin, Jean (Viator) 44 fig.37, 107 n.63

PERSPECTIVE
  accuracy 16–17, 44–5
  aerial 28, 102–3, 111 n.65
  angle of view see field of view
  angular 43, 44, 68–70, 104 n.12, 114
  apparent diameter 37, 39–40, 114
  appearance 41, 114
  bounded images 82, 93, 95–6, 100–1, 103 see also field of view
  centre point 64–5, 67, 114 see also viewpoint position, lateral
  and composition 63–6, 67–70, 82, 83, 88–9, 91, 93–4, 96, 102–3
  cone of vision 17, 36–7
  curved see non-standard
  curvilinear 38, 114
  distance, effect of see aerial
  distance point 114
  distance of view see viewpoint position
  distortion, 17–18, 40–3, 71–7
  eye see viewpoint
  eye/distance point 114
  field of view: circular 84, 91–2, 98–9, 100–1; limits of 42, 82, 84, 88, 91–2, 93, 95, 98–9, 110 n.63, 112 n.88, 112 n.99; peripheral 82, 100
  format of picture 77, 94, 95, 98, 99, 100 see also field of view
  frontal see parallel
  gradation see aerial
  horizon height 114 see also viewpoint position, height
  horizontal convergence see lateral convergence

lateral convergence 75–7
limits of view see field of view
linear see standard
marginal distortion 40–1 figs.32–6
measure point method 47, 57–8, 114
non-standard 71–4, 75–7, 83–4, 87–91, 92, 93 et seq., 110 n.62: light curved 50, 82–4
oblique see angular
panoramas 92, 111 n.82
parallel 43, 44, 55, 66, 67–70, 104 n.12, 114
peripheral vision see field of view
rectilinear 114
relevance to artists 17–18, 35–6, 38, 43, 62, 72–3, 83
standard 17, 36–7, 41–2, 82–3, 87, 96, 101, 103, 110 n.64, 114
value see relevance to artists
vanishing point 44, 114
vertical convergence 71–4
viewpoint position 114: distance 42, 72, 74, 77–82, 88, 100, 110 n.63, 112 n.88; height 54–5, 69–70, 74, 84, 85–7, 88–9; lateral position 64–5; lateral position, central 64–5, 67, 100–1
viewpoint, single fixed 17–18, 40–3, 79, 89–90, 92, 95, 99, 103, 114
vignettes see field of view, circular
wide angle see field of view

Piero della Francesca 109 n.22
Pilkington, Matthew 106 n.20
Pliny the Younger 19
Poussin, Nicholas 64, 68–9, 110 n.35
Pozzo, Andrea 44 fig.38, 107 nn.62, 63
Priestley, Joseph 92 fig.120

Raphael 23, 36, 44, 54–5 figs.54, 55, 68, 69, 85, 86, 87, 89, 105 n.49
Rembrandt 51
Repton, Humphry 98
Revett, Nicholas 106 n.11
Reynolds, Sir Joshua 16, 27, 35, 39, 53, 109 n.21
Rogers, Samuel 77, 100, 113 n.114
Rolls, William 105 n.26
Rooker, Michael Angelo 70
Royal Academy: Lecture Room (Great Room) 16 fig.2, 20, 23, 76 fig.94; lectures 27, 31, 104 nn.4, 24, 25, 105 n.28 see also Turner, as professor of perspective; lectures, audience for 15, 17
Rubens, Sir Peter Paul 43, 69
Ruskin, John 23, 62, 83, 98–100, 103, 110 n.63, 111 n.65

Scharf, George I 16 fig.2
Scheiner, Christopher 107 n.63
Scott, Sir Walter 90, 100
Sirigatti, Lorenzo 45–7, 47 fig.43, 107 n.63

[123]

INDEX

Soane, Sir John 27, 104 n.24, 104–5 n.25, 105 n.28
Stuart, James 106 n.11

Taylor, Brook 37, 38 fig.27, 104 nn.14, 20, 21, 107 n.37
Taylor, John 106 n.64
Thomson, James 105 n.30
Thornhill, Sir James 105 n.49
Titian 55 fig.56, 69
Troili, Guilio 107 n.63

TURNER, J.M.W.
'circular' pictures 98–9
and Claude 74, 81–2, 109 n.31
and Dürer 17 fig.5, 31 fig.16, 31–2, 34, 37, 44, 64, 104 n.17
and van Dyck 51, 53
and foreign languages 19
genius, views on 35
handwriting, etc. 14 fig.1, 22, 27, 28, 106 n.61
idealism 62, 103
lectures *see* as professor of perspective
perspective, ability in and knowledge of 28–9, 44–5, 57–63, 65–6, 85, 89–90, 103
  see also training, early
perspective, views on flaws in 40–3, 71–2, 75, 83–5, 102–3
perspective, views on importance of, general 33–4, 35–6, 38–9, 43, 45, 48, 63–4, 71–3, 83–4
  see also under PERSPECTIVE
and Poussin 68–9
as professor of perspective: election 15; performance as a lecturer 22–3, 26–8; preparation of lectures 18–21; research for lectures 19–20, 22, 32, 44, 106 n.20; revisions to lectures 21–2, 27, 28
and Raphael 23, 31, 36 fig.23, 44, 54–5 fig.55, 68, 69
and Rembrandt 51
and Reynolds 16, 35, 39, 53, 104 n.5, 107 n.26
and Rubens 43, 69
and Titian 55, 69
training, early 15, 58
vignettes 100–1, 110 n.62
vortices 96, 98–101

DRAWINGS
Cassiobury (TB CXX A, fig.65) 61
Christ Church, Oxford, Interior of the Hall at (TB L J, fig.63) 59–60
Ely Cathedral – The Interior of the Octagon (TB XXII P, fig.66) 61–2, 77, 110 n.63
Fonthill Abbey, South Front (TB XLVII 1, fig.89) 70
George IV at St Giles's, Edinburgh, Study for (TB CC f.33v., fig.117) 90, 91
George IV at St Giles's, Edinburgh, Study for (TB CC f.34, fig.118) 90, 91, 96
Little Chartreuse, Entrance to (TB LXXIV 24, fig.69) 64, 65, 100
Mountains beside a Lake (TB LXXIV 49, fig.101) 79
Naples with Vesuvius (TB CLXXXVII 14, fig.103) 80
New College, Oxford, Interior of the Chapel (TB L F, fig.64) 60–1

Pantheon, Oxford St (TB CXCV 156) 59, 105 n.45
Petworth Park (TB CCXLIII ff.77v., 78, fig.124) 92, 93
Petworth Park (CCCXLI 380, fig.125) 92, 93
Petworth Park (TB CCXLIII ff.76v., 77, fig.126) 93
Road from Voreppe to Grenoble (TB LXXIV 20, fig.72) 64–5
Rome from the Vatican, Study for (TB CLXXIX f.13v., fig.113) 86, 88
Rome from the Vatican, Study for (TB CLXXXIX 41, fig.114) 79, 86, 88, 96
Rome from the Vatican, Study for (TB CLXXIX f.26, fig.116) 89
Wanstead New Church (TB IV A) 58

LECTURE DIAGRAMS (and related works)
The Admiralty (TB CXCV 173, fig.22) 33
Brocklesby Mausoleum, Interior of (TB CXCV 130, fig.13) 23
Carlton House (TB CXCV 148, fig.21) 33
Colour Circle No.1 (TB CXCV 178, fig.10) 23
Conic and Cylindrical Sections (TB CXCV 62, fig.29) 39
Corinthian Capital in Perspective (TB CXCV 103, fig.46) 47, 48
Corinthian Capital, Perspective Construction of (TB CXCV 104, fig.47) 47, 48
Cross on a Cube, Perspective Study of (TB CXCV 158, fig.57) 57–8, 105 n.46, 108 n.3
Cross-sections of the Human Body (after Dürer) (TB CXCV 164, fig.16) 31–2
Doric Entablature, Perspective Study of (TB CXCV 98, fig.58) 58
Guidobaldo del Monte's Perspective Method for a Cube (TB CXCV 73, fig.6) 19
House, Perspective Construction of (TB CXCV 80, fig.40) 44–5, 108 n.7
House in Perspective (TB CXCV 82, fig.41) 44, 58
The Monument (TB CXCV 151, fig.18) 32
Objects Above, Level with, and Below, the Eye (TB CXCV 57, fig.25) 37
Parabola, Geometry of (TB CXCV 67, fig.30) 39
Perspective Method for a Rectangular Object, Basic (TB CXCV 79, fig.39) 44–5, 108 n.7
Perspective Method for a Square, attributed to '1505' (Jean Pelerin/Viator) (TB CXCV 71, fig.37) 44
Perspective, Standard, Geometry of (TB CXCV 2, fig.3) 17
Pozzo's Perspective Method (TB CXCV 78, fig.38) 44
Prison, Interior of (TB CXCV 120, fig.11) 23
Prison, Interior of (TB CXCV 121, fig.12) 23
Pulteney Bridge, Bath, Perspective Construction of (TB CXCV 113, fig.48) 47, 57, 58, 74, 108 n.6
Pulteney Bridge, Bath, in Perspective (TB CXCV 114, fig.49) 47, 58, 74, 108 n.6
Pulteney Bridge, Bath, Perspective Study of (TB CXCV 111, fig.59) 58, 108 nn.3, 6
Pulteney Bridge, Bath, in Perspective (tracing) (TB CXCV 112, fig.60) 58, 108 n.3
Raphael's 'St Paul Preaching at Athens',

Geometry of Figure of St Paul in (TB CXCV 168, fig.55) 55
Raphael's 'Transfiguration', Proportion and Design of (TB CXCV 163, fig.23) 31, 36, 105 n.49, 109 n.23
Real and Apparent Diameters of Spheres (TB CXCV 68, fig.31) 37, 40
Reflections in a Single Polished Metal Globe and a Pair of Polished Metal Globes (TB CXCV 176, fig.51) 53
Reflections in a Transparent Globe (TB CXCV 177A, fig.52) 53
Reflections and Refractions in Two Transparent Globes, One Half-filled with Water (TB CXCV 177C, fig.53) 53
Rows of Pillars Parallel and Close to the Picture Plane, Analysis of Perspective of (TB CXCV 69, fig.35) 41
Rows of Pillars and a Column Parallel and Close to the Picture Plane, Perspective Representation of (TB CXCV 146, fig.36) 41
St George's, Bloomsbury (TB CXCV 144, fig.20) 32, 74
St George's, Bloomsbury (TB CXCV 145, fig.92), 32, 73–4, 76
Sirigatti's Method for a Tuscan Capital (TB CXCV 85, fig.43) 45
Somerset House, Great Room (TB CXCV 70, fig.94) 43, 75, 76
Spheres at Different Distances from the Eye (TB CXCV 174, fig.24) 36–7
Temple of Neptune at Paestum (TB CXCV 102, fig.14) 23, 29
Terminology of Perspective of Thomas Malton Junior (TB CXCV 94, fig.28) 37
Terminology of Perspective of Moxon (TB CXCV 58, fig.26) 37
Terminology of Perspective of Brook Taylor (TB CXCV 59, fig.27) 37
Trajan's Column (TB CXCV 153, fig.17) 32
Triangles within Circles (TB CXCV 33, fig.9) 23
Tuscan Column in Perspective (TB CXCV 88, fig.44) 47, 49
Tuscan Column, Perspective Construction of (TB CXCV 90, fig.45) 47, 49

OIL PAINTINGS
Ancient Italy – Ovid Banished from Rome (B&J 375) 110 n.40
Ancient Rome (B&J 378) 110 n.40
Angel Standing in the Sun (B&J 425, fig.134) 99–100
Calais Pier (B&J 48, fig.77) 65
Caligula's Palace and Bridge (B&J 337) 110 n.40
The Decline of the Carthaginian Empire (B&J 135, fig.108) 69, 74, 81–2
Dido Building Carthage (B&J 131) 74
Forum Romanum, for Mr Soane's Museum (B&J 233, fig.105) 81
Frosty Morning (B&J 127, fig.78) 65
George IV at St Giles's, Edinburgh (B&J 247, fig.119) 90–1, 93
Juliet and her Nurse (B&J 365) 69
Light and Colour (Goethe's Theory) – The Morning after the Deluge – Moses

[124]

INDEX

Writing the Book of Genesis (B&J 405, fig.133) 98, 99
Modern Italy (B&J 374) 110 n.40
Modern Rome (B&J 379) 110 n.40
Palestrina – Composition (B&J 295, fig.79) 65
Parting of Hero and Leander (B&J 370, fig.97) 69, 77, 79, 111 n.80
Petworth Park: Tillington Church in the Distance (B&J 283, fig.121) 66, 79, 92–5, 98
Phryne Going to the Public Baths (B&J 373) 110 n.40
Rain, Steam and Speed (B&J 409) 69
Regulus (B&J 294, fig.87) 69, 74, 111 n.67, 113 n.113
Rome from the Vatican. Raffaelle, Accompanied by La Fornarina, Preparing his Pictures for the Decoration of the Loggia (B&J 228, fig.112) 85–90, 91, 93, 98, 113 n.112
Shade and Darkness – The Evening of the Deluge (B&J 404, fig.132) 66, 98, 99
The Tenth Plague of Egypt (B&J 17) 69

PRINTS
Fall of the Rebel Angels (fig.136) 100
Holy Island Cathedral (fig.90) 70
Isis (fig.82) 66
Loch Coriskin (fig.131) 96–7
Smailholm Tower 110 n.62

SKETCHBOOKS
Greenwich (TB CII) 105 n.25, 108 n.95
Grenoble (TB LXXIV) 64 fig.69, fig.72, 79 fig.101, 109 n.25
Perspective (TB CVIII) 17 fig.5, 19 fig.8, 37, 107 nn.32, 45, 108 n.85
Rome: C Studies (TB CLXXXIX) 86 fig.114
Studies for Pictures: Isleworth (TB XC) 109 n.25
Tivoli and Rome (TB CLXXIX) 86 fig.113, 89 fig.116
Windmill and Lock (TB CXIV) 32, 33 fig.19

WATERCOLOURS AND GOUACHES
Christ Church Cathedral, Oxford (TB VIII A) 109–10 n.9
Christ Church Cathedral, Oxford, Interior (TB L G, fig.95) 75–6
Dinant from the South-east (TB CCXX T, fig.129) 96
Ducal Palace: Porta della Carta, Venice (TB CCCXVIII 28, fig.91) 70
Eu, White Cliffs (TB CCCLIX 14, fig.102) 79–80
Evil Spirit (TB CCLXXX 202, fig.135) 100
Fall of the Clyde (Walker Art Gallery) 52
Figures in a Storm (TB CCCLXV 25, fig.86) 67
Glade and Greensward (TB CCXLIV 105, fig.127) 95
Goldau (TB CCCLXIV 281, fig.130) 96
Grand Canal, Venice: The Rialto, the Palazzo Balbi on the Left (TB CCCXV 20, fig.93) 74
Harfleur (TB CCLIX 86, fig.80) 66
Isola Bella, Lago Maggiore (TB CCLXXX 150, fig.98) 77, 100
Lausanne: Cathedral and Bridge (TB CCCXXXV 26, fig.84) 67, 100
Lausanne, Looking East (TB CCCXXXIV 3, fig.107) 81
Llandaff Cathedral: West Front (TB XXVIII A, fig.88) 70
Mainz (TB CCCLXIV 293, fig.67) 64, 65, 66
Bridge at Meulan (TB CCLIX 116, fig.81) 66
Palazzo Tasca-Papafava, Venice (TB CCCXVII 31, fig.73) 64
Pantheon Oxford Street, the Morning after the Fire (TB IX A, fig.62) 59, 70, 105 n.45
Sunset across Petworth Park (TB CCXLIV 2, fig.122) 93, 94, 95
Petworth Park: Sunset with a Cart (Mint Museum of Art, fig.123) 93, 94, 95
Promenade with Figures (TB CCCLXV 24, fig.68) 64
Radley Hall (TB III C, fig.61) 57, 58–9, 70
Rouen Cathedral (TB CCLIX 109, fig.106) 81
St Anne's Hill II (TB CCLXXX 171, fig.104) 80, 81
St Peter's, Rome, Part of the Portico (TB CLXXXIX 6, fig.96) 74, 76
Saumur (TB CCLIX 201, fig.111) 82
Pass of Splügen (TB CCCXXXVI 11, fig.70) 64, 100
Stangate Creek on the River Medway (TB CCVIII A, fig.83) 67
Town on the Loire (TB CCLIX 204, fig.110) 82
View across the Campagna with a Low Sun (TB CLXXXVII 43, fig.85) 67, 100
View on the Rhine or Neckar (TB CCCXLIX 27, fig.128) 96

Uccello, Paolo 34

Valenciennes, P.H. de 104 n.8
Vermeer, Jan 109 n.22
Viator *see* Pelerin, Jean
Vignola, Giacomo Barozzi da 107 nn.62, 63
Vredeman de Vries, Jan 104 n.17, 107 nn.62, 63

Wale, Samuel 104 nn.4, 15
Ware, Isaac 108 n.70
Westmacott, Sir Richard 16 fig.2
White, George Francis 109 n.15
Wilkie, David 107 n.23
Wilton, Joseph 48
Wood, John George 110 n.35
Wyatt, James 61, 63
Wyllie, W.L. 57

FRIENDS OF THE TATE GALLERY

Since their formation in 1958, the Friends of the Tate Gallery have helped to buy major works of art for the Tate Gallery Collection, from Stubbs to Hockney.

Members are entitled to immediate and unlimited free admission to Tate Gallery exhibitions with a guest, invitations to previews of Tate Gallery exhibitions, opportunities to visit the Gallery when closed to the public, a discount of 10 per cent in the Tate Gallery shop, special events, *Friends Events* and *Tate Preview* magazines mailed three times a year, free admission to exhibitions at Tate Gallery Liverpool, and use of the new Friends Room at the Tate Gallery, supported by Lloyd's of London.

Three categories of higher level memberships, Associate Fellow at £100, Deputy Fellow at £250, and Fellow at £500, entitle members to a range of extra benefits including guest cards and invitations to exclusive special events.

The Friends of the Tate Gallery are supported by Tate & Lyle PLC.

Further details on the Friends may be obtained from:

Friends of the Tate Gallery
Tate Gallery
Millbank
London SW1P 4RG
Tel: 071-821 1313 or 071-831 2742

Tate Gallery Liverpool Supporters

Tate Gallery Liverpool Supporters were established in 1989 to promote the Gallery and help raise funds for its exhibitions and projects.

Members are entitled to unlimited free admission to Tate Gallery Liverpool and London exhibitions, invitations to private previews of Tate Gallery Liverpool exhibitions, a discount of 10 per cent on Tate Gallery Liverpool catalogues and goods in the Tate Gallery London Shop, special events, invitations to the Supporters' annual party, regular information on all Tate Gallery Liverpool activities and *Tate Preview* magazine mailed three times a year.

Further details on the Supporters may be obtained from:

Tate Gallery Liverpool Supporters
Albert Dock
Liverpool L3 4BB
Tel: 051-709 3223

PATRONS OF THE TATE GALLERY

The Patrons of British Art support British painting and sculpture from the Elizabethan period through to the early twentieth century in the Tate Gallery's collection. They encourage knowledge and awareness of British art by providing an opportunity to study Britain's cultural heritage.

The Patrons of New Art support contemporary art in the Tate Gallery's collection. They promote a lively and informed interest in contemporary art and are associated with the Turner Prize, one of the most prestigious awards for the visual arts.

Annual membership of the Patrons ranges from £350 to £750, and funds the purchase of works of art for the Tate Gallery collection.

Benefits for both groups include invitations to Tate Gallery receptions, an opportunity to sit on the Patrons' acquisitions committees, special events including visits to private and corporate collections and complimentary catalogues of Tate Gallery exhibitions.

Further details on the Patrons may be obtained from:

The Development Office
Tate Gallery
Millbank
London SW1P 4RG
Tel: 071-821 1313

SPONSORSHIP

Tate Gallery, London – Sponsorships since 1989

Agfa Graphic Systems Group
 1991, *Turner: The Fifth Decade* exhibition and catalogue
Barclays Bank PLC
 1991, *Constable* exhibition
Beck's
 1992, *Otto Dix* exhibition
British Gas North Thames
 1989, *Colour into Line: Turner and the Art of Engraving* exhibition
British Gas plc
 1989, Education study sheets
The British Land Company PLC
 1990, *Joseph Wright of Derby* exhibition
The British Petroleum Company plc
 1989, *Paul Klee* exhibition
 1990–3, *New Displays*
British Steel plc
 1989, *William Coldstream* exhibition
Carroll, Dempsey & Thirkell
 1990, *Anish Kapoor* exhibition
Channel 4 Television
 1991–3, The Turner Prize
Clifton Nurseries
 1989–91, Sponsorship in kind
Daimler-Benz AG
 1991, *Max Ernst* exhibition
Debenham Tewson & Chinnocks
 1990, Turner *Painting and Poetry* exhibition
Digital Equipment Co Ltd
 1991, *From Turner's Studio* touring exhibition
Drivers Jonas
 1989, *Turner and Architecture* exhibition
Erco Lighting
 1989, Sponsorship in kind
The German Government
 1992, *Otto Dix* exhibition
The Independent
 1992, *Otto Dix* exhibition
KPMG Management Consulting
 1991, *Anthony Caro: Sculpture towards Architecture* exhibition
Lin Pac Plastics
 1989, Sponsorship in kind
Linklaters & Paines
 1989, Japanese Guide to Turner Bequest
Lloyd's of London
 1991, Friends Room

Olympia & York
 1990, Frameworkers Conference
PA Consulting Group
 1989, Video projector
Pearson plc
 1992–5, Elizabethan Curator Post
Reed International P.L.C.
 1990, *On Classic Ground* exhibition
SRU Ltd
 1989, Market research consultancy
 1992, *Richard Hamilton* exhibition
Tate & Lyle PLC
 1991–3, Friends relaunch marketing programme
TSB Group plc
 1992, *Turner and Byron* exhibition
 1992–5, *William Blake* series of displays
Ulster Television plc
 1989, *F.E. McWilliam* exhibition
Volkswagen
 1989–92, The Turner Scholarships
Westminster City Council
 1989, Trees project
 1989, *The Tate Gallery Companion* (New Display guidebook)

Tate Gallery Liverpool – Sponsorships since 1989

AIB Bank
 1991, *Strongholds* exhibition
Barclays Bank PLC
 1990, *New Light on Sculpture* display
BASF
 1990, *Lifelines* exhibition
Beck's Bier
 1990, *Art from Köln* exhibition
British Alcan Aluminium plc
 1991, *Dynamism* display
 1991, *Giacometti* display
British Telecom plc
 1989, Salary for media van
 1990, Outreach Programme
Concord Lighting
 1990, Sponsorship in kind
Cultural Relations Committee, Department of Foreign Affairs, Ireland
 1991, *Strongholds* exhibition
English Estates
 1991, Mobile Arts Project
Granada Television plc
 1990, *New North* exhibition
Korean Air
 1992, Sponsorship in kind
The Littlewoods Organisation plc
 1992–5, *New Realities* display
Merseyside Development Corporation
 1990, Outreach programme
 1992, *Myth-Making* display
 1992, *Stanley Spencer* display
Mobil Oil Company Ltd
 1990, *New North* exhibition
Momart plc
 1989–92, Artist's Fellowship at Tate Gallery Liverpool
NSK Bearings Europe Ltd
 1991, *A Cabinet of Signs* exhibition
Pentagram Design Limited
 1991, Sponsorship in kind
Ryanair
 1991, Sponsorship in kind
Samsung Electronics
 1992, *Working with Nature* exhibition
Tate Gallery Liverpool Supporters
 1991–2, An events programme
Volkswagen
 1991, Sponsorship in kind

TATE GALLERY, LONDON – CORPORATE MEMBERS

Partners

Agfa UK Ltd
Barclays Bank PLC
The British Petroleum Company plc
Glaxo Holdings p.l.c.
Manpower (UK) Ltd
THORN EMI
Unilever

Associates

Bell Helicopter Textron
Channel 4 Television
Debenham Tewson & Chinnocks
Ernst & Young
KPMG Peat Marwick
Lazard Brothers & Co Ltd
Linklaters & Paines
Smith & Williamson
Vickers plc
S.G. Warburg Group